FATHERS OF THE CHURCH

FATHERS OF THE CHURCH

Donald W. Wuerl

Our Sunday Visitor, Inc.
Huntington, Indiana 46750

Nihil Obstat:
Rev. Lawrence Gollner
Censor Librorum

Imprimatur:
✝Leo A. Pursley, D.D.
Bishop of Fort Wayne-South Bend
December 15, 1974

The Nihil Obstat and Imprimatur are official declarations that a book or pamphlet is free of doctrinal or moral error. No implication is contained therein that those who have granted the Nihil Obstat or Imprimatur agree with the contents, opinions or statements expressed.

ISBN: 0-87973-765-4
Library of Congress Catalog Card Number: 75-4062

Cover Design by James E. McIlrath
Photo Courtesy Ringling Museum of Art

Second Printing, 1977

Published, printed and bound in the U.S.A. by
Our Sunday Visitor, Inc.
Noll Plaza
Huntington, Indiana 46750

765

CONTENTS

PREFACE

With all the profusion of public personalities and with the richness of theologians to the point of embarrassment with which our generation has been endowed, why a book looking back sixteen centuries and more to stimulate contemporary interest in the lives and thought of men so remote in Christian history as the Church Fathers?

Perhaps the answer lies in the premise of the question. Quite possibly the very questions of our times are those to which our Fathers in the faith addressed themselves. Perhaps under their grey beards they were tempted by the same heresies and sustained by the same truths as are our most recent but not necessarily more profound scholars who are the beneficiaries of developed but unchanged data of faith in their theological speculations.

Perhaps, too, the premise is false. Possibly we are too prone to divide the history of the Church into past, present and future; our vocabulary sometimes suggests as much. The Church, the beginning on earth of the Kingdom of Heaven, shares something of that Eternal Now in which all the people of God are in the essential things more close to one another than details of space or time may indicate.

But even in the face of the centuries that separate us from the Fathers of the Church, the reasons for cultivating knowledge and reverence are many and powerful. The first is *spiritual piety*. The Fathers of the Church are our ancestors in the faith, the remote founders of the Christian heritage that is ours. All men are bound to their ancestors by the gratitude and reverence that is *piety,* the virtue that links us to our origins as does family piety, patriotic piety, even the piety we owe to God.

Then there is the consideration of intellectual profit. Professor E. K. Rand, in his *Founders of the Middle Ages,* records the description of Migne's *Patrologia,* the collected works of the Fathers of the Church, as a *five-fathom* bookshelf, as contrasted with the five-foot bookshelf marketed a couple of generations ago. A more devastating contrast could be made as between the volumes of patristic literature and, say, the Book-of-the-Month clubs or the "spiritual and theological current classics" made available, at reasonable prices, by contemporary publishing houses in print or on cassettes. This is not to deny the value of all the insights of the new thought; it is simply to put matters in perspective by recalling that, in theology as in warfare, there were many brave men before Agamemnon's time. And of these, the greatest and the most rewarding were the Fathers of the Church.

Finally, reading the patristic authors, one reflects frequently on how much they bring both to the statement and the solution of the problems concerning God and Man that we like to think of as peculiarly modern. It would be difficult to think of a heresy or excess of recent decades that does not find its statement in the age of the Fathers. *Tertullian* was alarmed by the "exploding population" of over six-

8

teen centuries ago that had so over-peopled the earth as to outstrip our resources for survival. Origen had his doubts about the Devil and the eternity of hell. The rhetoric of twentieth-century, polarized leftists and rightists can be found in some of the writings of even the best of the Fathers and among them (think only of Jerome and Augustine) there was a sometimes astonishing amount of that frank, sincere and courageous confrontation (dialogue!) that we liked to think of as postconciliar and characteristic of our so improved times and intelligences.

But much more important is the contribution the Fathers of the Church have to make to our vital, profound understanding of the ever-ancient, ever-new crises, contradictions and ultimate truths which fascinate, trouble or inspire us still. And so, if it is important to listen, carefully but critically, to what "the theologians are telling us," it is vastly more so to reflect knowledgeably on what the Fathers of the Church still say to us by word and example.

Father Wuerl has done a great service to knowledge and wisdom, not always found in one another's company, by his popular but informed presentation of the memories and the mind of some of the Church Fathers. May his book be but a prelude to a grassroots revival of profit, pleasure and holy pride in the Fathers of the Church and the Church of the Fathers whose children we are, or we are orphans.

✠ John Cardinal Wright

Clement, Ignatius and Polycarp

THE FIRST FATHERS

They (the Apostles) appointed such men, and made provision that, when these men should die, other approved men would take up their ministry.

—*St. Clement of Rome*
'Letter to the Corinthians'

Before the first fifty years had passed since the crucifixion of Christ, the whole religious world of the Middle East was changed. When Jesus was led to Calvary, His followers were few and their leadership disorganized. The civil jurisdiction of Jerusalem was a tangled, confused web of Roman law and Jewish regulations. The Roman procurator and the ancient Hebrew Sanhedrin claimed areas of jurisdiction. Jerusalem could boast of being, after Rome itself, the largest city within the Empire. But all this was soon changed. What Emperor Vespasian had begun, his

11

son and heir Titus completed in the siege and capture of Jerusalem in the year 70. Those Jewish people who remained from the rage of slaughter were deported, the Temple destroyed, the city razed. Testimony to this tragic event can be vividly seen in Rome marked by the Arch of Titus in the Roman forum.

Against this background, the new faith — belief in the risen Christ — spread. Most of those who had looked on the face of the Lord died far from the familiar sights of Judea and Galilee. As these Apostles and disciples moved, they carried the faith, founded communities and preached the word. They were aided in all of this by a network of Roman highways that crisscrossed the then known world. Over all 55,000 miles of this enormous paving project the disciples traveled. Soon Paul was dashing off letters to his fledgling churches as he made his way back and forth across what is now Greece and Turkey, until he finally ended up in Rome. Peter reached the same city — the heart, soul and mind of the Empire — and set up his teaching chair.

The letters that we have that come from the Apostles are found in the New Testament. Those writings sent to various churches by Paul, Peter, John, James and Jude are revered as inspired. But they were not the only ones writing. Before the century was finished, a whole group of bishops were instructing, encouraging, teaching and admonishing their flocks and fellow-believers via the mails. Perhaps the fact that the mails then were not much better than they are now accounts for so many of these letters having been lost.

These writers who followed in the footsteps of the Apostles have come to be known as the apostolic

Fathers. The name simply notes that they were writing within the lifetime of some of the Apostles or their immediate successors and convert disciples. While St. John was still alive and writing, three men had followed Peter as Bishop of Rome. One of these has left a very important letter with which we will begin our study of the apostolic Fathers.

St. Clement came to the Chair of Peter after the death of Pope Cletus in the year 90. Cletus had labored to call attention to the spiritual treasure that Rome had in its possession in the tomb of the Prince of the Apostles. He had as early as the year 82 built an oratory over the burial place of Peter. This place already had become a spot of pilgrimage among the Christians in Rome and visiting believers.

What we know about Clement is found in some of the ancient writers of later centuries. Origen and Eusebius both assert that Clement was the so-called "fellow-worker" mentioned by St. Paul when he was writing to the Philippians. Eusebius was a great historian of the ancient Church — possibly its greatest. His testimony is particularly valuable.

Other writers of this same period list Clement as the third successor to Peter as Bishop of Rome. And his name is found in the ancient list of Popes compiled by Irenaeus. He seems to have served as a sort of auxiliary bishop for the two Popes who followed St. Peter: Linus and Cletus. His own years of service as the Servant of the Servants of God lasted nine years. He finally died under the Emperor Trajan in 99 A.D. The brief span of his years in Rome as head of the Church there saw the reign of three emperors. Domitian, who was the brother of Titus, was emperor when Clement took over the job as Bishop of

Rome. He was followed by Nerva, whose reign was really a short interlude of an interloper. Clement died while Trajan was busy expanding the limits of the imperial holdings to their farthest extent.

To this day there is still living testimony to Clement of Rome in the Eternal City. St. Clement's Church, which is now, as it has been for 400 years, administered by the Irish Dominican Fathers, is the resting place of the earthly remains of this ancient hero of Rome. This church is of particular interest to Americans because its ancient structure and precious mosaics were restored by Cardinal William O'Connell, Archbishop of Boston, and the present titular pastor of that Church is the recently retired Archbishop of Baltimore, Cardinal Shehan.

What we have of the writings of St. Clement is one letter. He wrote to the Corinthians. Apparently, the Corinthians were always acting up. Either they were in schism or fighting among themselves. St. Paul wrote to them a strong letter reminding them of their obligations in charity. The schism seems to have gotten much worse. Clement writes to them a very strong letter. He takes them to task for their independence in matters of faith. The Corinthians, as citizens of one of the great trading centers of the ancient world, considered themselves highly independent individuals. We read even in the Acts of the Apostles how they could easily be stirred up particularly when their financial interests were touched. It was a sort of trading center with a bad reputation.

Much like St. Paul, Clement appeals to charity, and he pleads that their divisions not become a cause of scandal within the Church.

Aside from the priestly concern of St. Clement,

his letter offers remarkable testimony to the mind and condition of the ancient Church. Clement is writing as Bishop of Rome. Under that title he does not hestiate to correct, rebuke and order other churches. He makes no justification for his intervention in the internal affairs of Corinth other than that he is Bishop of Rome. Corinth is in confusion and the faith is being deluded. Clement sees it as his job, duty and right to set things straight.

Since we date this letter some time in the 90s, we are led to assume that St. John — the well-beloved disciple of Jesus — was still alive. Yet the appeal is to Clement, not John. Clement is now the voice of Peter, the Chair of Rome. The principle at issue in the fight at Corinth is of less concern to us today than the manner in which it was settled. From St. Clement's letter of intervention, we have proof from the earliest days of the apostolic Church that the weight and authority of the Bishop of Rome was recognized, respected and undisputed. This, of course, makes it difficult to assert that the Roman prerogatives were later additions growing out of the confusion of the Dark Ages and the political significance of a restored Roman authority in the high Middle Ages.

This letter and the manner of its instruction shows us another fact about the structure of the Church in its earliest days. It was a hierarchical church. St. Clement speaks very clearly of the role of bishops and deacons within the Church. And in an amazingly forthright statement he points out that bishops receive their authority from Christ through the Apostles and not "out of the community." The distinction of a hierarchical church versus a democratic church was clear to St. Clement. Apparently, it was not disputed by those who received his letter, and certainly not in Rome itself. Clement writes that the hierarchical structure of the Church is received directly from Jesus Christ. He points out that all authority within the Church is channeled through the apostolic succession. He is quite explicit in noting that bishops were appointed by the Apostles when the Apostles knew that they were to die and that others would carry on their work. Mind you, all of this is taking place before the end of the first century of the Christian era.

Another enlightening piece of doctrine found in this letter of St. Clement is the role of sacrifice in priestly activity. Clement stresses that the unique principle of priestly duty is to offer the sacrifice of the Mass.

The importance of the testimony of St. Clement for the Church is very simply that it was given at the most only fifty years after Christ's death. There was not time for new inventions to be introduced that could have so distorted Christ's message as to render Clement a fraud. The transmission of fact as Christ and the Apostles saw it is part of the uniqueness of Clement's testimony. There was not time for confusions to intervene. We might say by way of parallel that it is almost as if a historian today were to write about World War I and the founding of the League of Nations. His sources and witnesses would still be very fresh. In some instances, living witnesses would be there to contradict any wild falsification such as, for example, that the Kaiser and Germany were not defeated. So important is Clement's testimony because of its antiquity that it has always been held in great veneration in the Church.

Eusebius, the historian, sensed the great importance of Clement's testimony. A living continuity between the Apostles and Clement existed. His letter was not classroom theorizing. It was not the tentative ideas of a guest lecturer. It was witness to something of which he was a living, breathing part. Eusebius writes:

"He (Clement) had seen the blessed Apostles and conversed with them, and still had the teaching of the Apostles ringing in his ears and their tradition before his eyes. He was not alone in this, for many were still alive at the time who had been taught by the Apostles" (*Ecclesiastical History,* Book 5, Ch. 6).

Cardinal Danielou writes that Clement is the "heir" to the tradition of St. Peter and St. Paul at Rome. He also points out another interesting fact about the life of the Church at the time of Clement. When Clement quotes the words of Christ he does not use the written Gospels. He quotes from an oral tradition. Danielou notes: "This does not mean that the written Gospels were unknown to our author, but that Christ's teaching was transmitted both in writing and in catechetical tradition." This fact again points out the existence of a living tradition in the Church.

Rome was not the only city with a living tradition kept intact by the faith of the community and the presence of a bishop. Antioch in Greece and Smyrna in Asia Minor (the area of modern Turkey) are other examples of the rapid spread of the Church and its formation around the bishop-teacher.

Within the same period of time we also find as Bishop of Antioch St. Ignatius. Unfortunately, we do not know as much about Ignatius as we do of Clement, even though their bones rest together in the same church in Rome. Most of what we know about Ignatius comes from his seven letters. These "precious treasures" of early Christian literature were written as he made his way from Antioch to Rome — under a death sentence. Eusebius, our ancient historian, says that he was the third Bishop of Antioch. This implies that he followed immediately after the man who succeeded St. Peter himself. Ignatius fell under the death sentence for professing the faith some time before the close of the century. As he traveled to Rome a prisoner, he wrote his letters explaining the faith, teaching and exhorting as he went along. He seems at length to have died in the Flavian amphitheater at Rome. In this huge building, called today the Colosseum, numerous Christians died. The death of Ignatius, though barbaric, was not unusual as applied to Christians, criminals and dissidents of the day.

The Emperor Trajan had enlarged his empire so that it ran from Scotland to the borders of Persia, and from the Black Sea to the west coast of Africa. Everywhere the Roman eagle ruled. But it had some awful side effects for Rome. The city on the Tiber swelled by the influx of slaves, merchants and freebooters until its population rapidly reached a million. These crowds — whom the Romans called rabble — had to be kept happy. This grew into the well-known "bread and circuses" routine which saw many a Christian used as live bait for the wild animals in the so-called games. Ignatius apparently perished in one of these spectacles.

His letters, however, remain a testimony to the depth of his learning and grasp of the faith. It almost seems inconceivable, even when we make allowance for the normal development of doctrine and discipline within the life of the Church, that so much of its teaching was so clearly grasped by Ignatius before the first century of the new era was out. In what amounted to four score and seven years after the death of Christ, Ignatius was writing on the Trinity, the Incarnation, the Redemption and the Eucharist. His view of the hierarchy of the bishop, priest and deacon within the structured Church is clear. He sees the center of the Church as Rome, and the opposite pole of this universal Church, the local bishop and, therefore, local church. Ignatius stresses the universality of the Church. She reaches out to all men and makes room for all men in her fold. Another interesting subject touched on by Ignatius is that of the value of consecrated virginity. He points out, as does St. Paul, that this sacrifice is in reality a beautiful sign of the coming Kingdom of God.

Writing to the Magnesians, Ignatius tells them that the office of bishops is worthy of not just respect but obedience. The Church there apparently had a young bishop whose age made his teaching with authority a bit difficult. Ignatius writes:

"It ill becomes you to treat your bishop too familiarly because of his age. You should show him all reverence out of respect for the authority of God the Father. This, I understand, the holy priests do . . . they yield to him as to one who is wise in God."

On the same theme to the Church of the Trallians he says:

"Do nothing apart from the bishop. Be obedient, too, to the priests as to the Apostles of Jesus Christ . . . and in the same way all should respect the deacons."

What makes this line of thought more relevant

today is the fact that Ignatius, besides seeing sacerdotal offices as ones enjoying authority, is taking for granted that all the others in the Churches to which he writes are already familiar with the hierarchical structure as if it had always been so established.

To the Romans he writes that they should not be surprised if he is to die at the hands of the civil authorities. Much more so he tells them not to try to interfere with his end. He teaches them that there will always be a conflict between those who live by the spirit and those who see only this world. He carries on this theme in the "Letter to the Philadelphians" where he tells them to beware of the powers of this political order who would with "tricks and traps" make this world out to be the only worthy motive for living. As did Christ, Ignatius teaches that the Kingdom of God is not of this world.

His letters to the Ephesians, Magnesians, the Trallians, Romans, Philadelphians, Smyrnians and to Polycarp could, with little change, be addressed to their modern-day counterparts. They would still be found up-to-date as far as the subject matter goes and would seem quite relevant to any discussion today. In the letter to the Ephesians, for example, we find Ignatius exhorting the believer to set an example so that the faith will be seen by others and will be attractive to them. He warns against "some outsiders" wandering about teaching bad doctrine. He is aware of the problem of keeping a constant and clear doctrine in the face of numerous personal interpretations.

He lists three "resounding mysteries" that are seen and understood only by those humble before the word and actions of God: the virginity of Mary, the Incarnation, the death of Christ. These three doctrinal positions alone warrant the praise that has been heaped on the letters of St. Ignatius. When we again consider that he is writing within a hundred years of Christ's death, we can appreciate the enormous value of his statements. The doctrinal solidification is so quick that it is very hard to challenge the source.

Ignatius' writing on the role of bishops in the Church might well seem to be themes taken from the Vatican Council or the Third Synod of Bishops. Ignatius is convinced that the center of the Church, that is, the local community of believers, is the bishop. He is the source of unity and the principal celebrant of the sacred mysteries. Today when we read that this position is an invention more of Vatican Council II and the Third Synod of Bishops we find that a quick leapfrog back over 1,800 years gives us Ignatius' doctrine, which is identical to that being taught by the Church today. Ignatius says that "there be nothing among you to divide you but be at one with your bishops and with those who are over you, thus affording of a model and a lesson on immortal life" (Magnesians, 6). In the theology of Ignatius, the unity of the Church is based on the immortal life that the Father sent to man through His Son. Ignatius sees a beautiful picture of the Father sending the Son, who in turn sends the Church in the person of bishops to carry His words, life and love to all the faithful. The same picture was used in the Third Synod by one of the Fathers in his description of the Church. In fact, the Synod document uses Ignatius without, however, giving him credit.

Ignatius based his faith — and a strong one it was — on the fact that Jesus Christ had risen from the dead in the flesh. This was the cornerstone of his belief. "As for me I know that even after His Resurrection He was in the flesh, and I believe this to be true" (Smyrnians, 3). It was this faith that he taught and it was this faith that sustained him.

Ignatius' last letter was addressed to Polycarp, and this saint was soon to follow Ignatius on the road to martyrdom. Indeed, the martyrdom of Polycarp, an authentic account of his heroic and Christian end, forms part of the literature of the apostolic Church. Polycarp was a well-known and esteemed person in the first half of the second century of the Christian era. Tertullian, Irenaeus and Eusebius say that Polycarp was instructed in the faith by none other than John the Apostle. If this be so, we can imagine a young convert sitting at the feet of an old and yet very much alive man somewhere in the Christian sector of Ephesus. We can envision this young man coming alive with the excitement of the tale of Jesus' life, death and Resurrection as he hears it from a man who not only looked upon the face of Jesus but walked with Him after he had seen Him die. Polycarp, so we are told by Tertullian, went to Smyrna, where he is now venerated as the first bishop. Today, the present Bishop of Izmir, which is the city standing alongside what is left of the ruins of Smyrna, is an American. Archbishop John Boccella signs himself Bishop of Izmir, Successor of Polycarp. It is very hard to find a more ancient title within the Catholic communion.

In writing on St. Polycarp's "Letter to the Phillippians," Glimm notes that at least part of the letter would have been written while St. Ignatius was still on his way to Rome for trial or, before St. Polycarp had received any news of his death. This means that

22

the letter, in substance, is dated prior to the year 110 A.D.

Even this early in the life of the Church there were internal problems. Not everyone was keeping to the spirit and letter of the Gospel traditions. Some claimed a deeper knowledge of the truth and of the meaning of the faith than was given to the "common masses of the believers." Others relied on personal visions and revelations to supplement the Spirit given to the rest of the Church. In the first case we have a heresy called "Gnosticism." The latter incident that recurs regularly is called "Montanism."

Both excesses in the spiritual life of the Church gnawed at her vital energies. One divided the Church into those who "really know what it is all about" and the "simple old-fashioned believer." One cut the community of believers into those who merely lived the life of Christ and those who have "truly" received the Spirit. Perhaps this explains, in part, Ignatius' insistence on the conformity of faith and practice with the ancient and living traditions of the Church.

Polycarp offers us an interesting testimony on the canon of the New Testament. Already by the time Polycarp was teaching and writing, certain works of the Apostles were considered the inspired Word of God. We see Polycarp writing to the Philippians quoting the Acts of the Apostles, the Letter of Peter, the Epistles to the Ephesians, the Epistles to the Corinthians, the Gospel of St. Matthew and many other works that are part of the New Testament. Indirectly, Polycarp is confirming for us that the words of the Gospel and Paul that were written and sent to individual churches were diffused rapidly throughout the whole believing world.

The theology of Polycarp in his one epistle is a masterpiece of incarnational theology. Polycarp insists that Jesus Christ in the flesh lived, died and rose. He goes into the tale to emphasize the importance of the flesh aspect of Christ. His is a confession of Christ's physical presence, historical role and real resurrection. In this he certainly follows the teaching of St. Paul.

The question of what Easter means was first answered by St. Paul in one of the earliest expressions of the Church's teaching. Paul was writing to the Corinthians. And for him the risen Lord was the heart and soul of Christianity. And the risen Lord necessarily implies a resurrection. In writing to the Corinthians Paul apparently was attempting to settle some of the problems revolving around the question of the risen body. Paul does not seem to face any challenge on the fact that Christ is risen. In fact, he presents this as the accepted Gospel message — accepted also at Corinth: "I handed on to you the facts which had been imparted to me, that Christ died for our sins, . . . was buried, that He was raised to life on the third day" (1 Corinthians 15:3-4).

Interestingly, in this earliest formula of faith we see listed the fact that Christ was dead and bodily buried. His death was not symbolic nor was there question about the fact that He was committed to the grave as are all the dead. This one phrase "was buried" is not without significance alongside the next line that reads, "He was raised to life." For St. Paul the continuity of Christ's life-death-risen life is an established fact. The same Christ, in the flesh, who hanged on Calvary, was anointed for burial, and rose from the dead. The same teaching is found in Polycarp's writings with perhaps an additional emphasis.

Polycarp's death was, again, a martyrdom. He was arrested in Rome and sentenced by the proconsul to death on charges of *lèse majesté* — refusing to worship Caesar. I suppose today Polycarp would be looked upon as a very uncompromising soul. For even in the face of the compromise worked out by the proconsul, Polycarp stood fast. The proconsul had offered an oath by which Polycarp could seem to be swearing by the genius of Caesar and thus avoid a head-on confrontation. Polycarp preferred to die than to mingle the faith in outright compromise.

These few excerpts from three ancient writers only scratch the surface of the doctrine and importance of the apostolic Fathers. However, they do present a picture of the Church that we can readily recognize today. The startling fact is that they were writing about the Church at its very birth nearly 2,000 years ago.

Justin
the Martyr

It is for us, therefore, to offer to all the opportunity of inspecting our life and teachings, lest we ourselves should bear the blame for what those who do not really know about us do in their ignorance.

— *St. Justin*
'First Apology' (No. 3)

Between the years 70 and 150, the Catholic faith grew in various parts of the Mediterranean world. As it did so, it began to express differences in many ways. The Church in Armenia, Syria, as well as in Asia Minor, developed its own tradition. The Church in Rome was also building its own practices. From the center — Rome — these customs were soon to spread throughout the Western world, becoming the Latin Rite. On the periphery of the Church, however, theological aberrations began to creep in. These, what we

26

would call heresies, have names that ring with an odd sound today. Some were called Gnostics, others Montanists, and still another group, the Ebionites. With their own version of Christ's message, they were to present a problem to the united Church. As in every case, a heresy is an exaggeration. It settles on one aspect of the faith and blows it out of proportion. Soon this lopsided doctrine becomes the only doctrine.

The confusion occasioned a new type of Christian literature. This style of writing, to correct errors or more often to convert to the faith, came to be called "apologetics." This literature was necessitated as the Church grew. More people began to look at it. Those outside the Church were sometimes very hostile to an institution they did not understand. Thus, this animosity increased as conflicting stories about the Church's doctrines spread. In reply to all of this, apologetics came into existence. The first noted writer of this type was St. Justin.

With St. Justin, our look at the Church Fathers moves into the second century of the Christian era. According to the venerated Church historian Eusebius, Justin was born somewhere between 100 and 110 A.D. His birthplace was a town in Samaria, the area to the north of Judea and Jerusalem in the Holy Land. After the Roman legions at the orders of Vespasian and Titus had reduced Jerusalem to rubble, they set about redoing the political boundaries of all of Palestine. They rebuilt towns and cities. Much like Tiberius who had the city on the shores of Lake Galilee named after himself, so Vespasian of the Flavian family built a town and named it Flavia Neapolis (Flavian's New City). The city was built over the ruins of Sichen, the one-time capital of Samaria. Here Justin first saw the light of day.

What we know about Justin has to be pieced together from various sources and writers. We are told that he was a Roman citizen. If this be true, then Justin certainly came from a "good" family. Roman citizenship in those days was a treasured item. St. Paul was able to use his citizenship to invoke a privilege that exempted him from trial by anyone else than the emperor himself. Justin was living after St. Paul, but certainly before this privilege had been diluted by being extended to just about everybody.

We are told that Justin studied in Greece. This is another reason for us to assume that he came from a family that was fairly well-off. All the "best people" at that time studied in Athens. No upper-class education was considered complete unless the young and budding scholar had crossed from Italy into the land of the ancients to study the classics. The attraction is somewhat similar to the present-day practice of sending students to Europe.

While in Greece, the young Justin would have studied logic, philosophy, literature, and have come into contact with many of the leading currents of thought that swept the Mediterranean world. He would have also run headlong into the predominant humanistic literature of the day. Plato and the other great philosophers of antiquity would have been the "heady" drink of Justin the student.

It was while getting his formal education that Justin first came into contact with Christian theories and ideals. In his *Dialogue,* which he was to write later, he speaks about his conversion. He tells us that he was trying to form a perfect idea of God and how he eventually came to Christ. In this *Dialogue* he writes: "A long time ago, long before the time of those reputed philosophers, there lived blessed men, just and loved by God, men who spoke through the inspiration of the Holy Spirit and predicted events that would come to pass in the future, which events are now taking place. We call those men prophets. Their writings are still extant, and whoever reads them with proper faith will profit greatly and his knowledge of the origin and the end of things, and of any other matter that a philosopher should know. Thus, above all, you should beseech God to open to you the gates of light, for no one can perceive or understand these truths unless he has been enlightened by God and His Christ" (*Dialogue with Trypho,* Ch. 7).

Justin tells us there was another major reason for his conversion. This reason was a practical one. He saw Christians and admired them. He says that he was so impressed by their conduct that he wanted to learn more about them. Eusebius writes that when Justin heard the Christians misrepresented or watched them stand fearless in the face of death, he realized that there must be something to what they were talking about. We do not have an exact date for Justin's conversion. But some of the writers from antiquity tell us that it was probably 130 A.D. At this time he entered into a lifetime campaign to bring others to the faith.

Justin offers to the world today an outstanding example of a layman who is eager to share his belief with others, particularly in that area of competence in which he feels comfortable. Justin was of a good family, well-educated and at home with philosophical discussions and theological debates. It was natural for him after his conversion to use these talents to bring others to the Church.

Justin was convinced that conversion demands witness. He was equally convinced that every believer must actively tell other people about the faith. He was an apologist. And this essentially is what an apologist does. He acts as a witness — someone who tells others about Christ.

The function of the witness is indispensable to the faith and this missionary task. There can be no diffusion of the Kingdom of God unless those called to live in the Kingdom tell others of it. Since no one can see the Kingdom or supernatural realities that ground it, they have to be told of them. Grace, life eternal, redemption are not to be known unless one hears of them. They cannot be discovered as they were revealed unless those who have received the "good news" of them are willing to tell others of them. The witness must, then, testify to the content of his faith, since it is the "world of faith" within which he lives.

The witness of Christ will stand in relation to the faith as Christ stood in relation to the mystery of His Father in its revelation. To testify to the faith is to participate in the revealing action of the Incarnate Christ who spoke for the Father. The believer shares in that ministry of spreading the knowledge of God. But that witness must participate in the limitation that is Incarnation. The Son of God could use only human words, signs and institutions to reach men with His news of the Father and life in His presence. Human words, signs and structures must continue the work of Christ's revelation. The limitations of in-

30

dividual witness become apparent. Each believer who is prepared to testify to Christ's Kingdom among men must do so in order and with signs that are understood among men. He cannot claim to have or impart a directly received understanding of the Kingdom. His faith also is a received one. Therefore, his testimony must reflect the testimony as given by the entire community of believers. Cooperation in action and unity in mission must be the signs of the witness-missionary. In this manner, each individual gives his testimony in the larger context of the living witness of the Church.

The foremost means instituted to pass on the self-revelation by God is the Church. To the Church is given the full office of testifying to all the works of God. In this sense the Church can claim to be the only witness to Christ. She was created to be Christ's extension in the world. Her members share His life, His mission, His function in their faith. Yet their role is mediated by the Church. Only in and through her can they authentically and fully witness Christ. As the Church is the first to participate in Christ's redemptive action in the world, so does each believer through his membership in the Church participate in the same mission. The individual claim to witness is specifically as a member of the Church. His mission is received through her.

The primacy of the collective witness of the community does not in any way minimize the witness value of each member. The nature of witness requires that it be specifically personal. But at the same time it must be part of a larger context. The personal witness of the believer is thus able to impart the truth — the faith. Each Christian is called to be a witness of the

31

faith. His testimony is to be the instrument that leads others to the life of the faith and confirms those already living it. St. James writes of the need that faith be practical. It must bear fruit. We are to be doers of the word not just hearers (James 1:26). Witness must be worked out in very real concrete situations. Practical faith demands concrete witness (James 2:14-19). The Gospels note the very simple form in which love becomes living witness. "If you love me you will keep my commandments" (John 14:15). When the words of faith and the obligations of love take on flesh in their concrete realization, then they become at the same time living witness.

Rome understood little of what the apologist wrote. But it still continued to be the center of the world. Everything depended on this one city. So naturally, after his education, he returned to Rome. Much like the old town meetings in the United States, the Roman forum and its baths offered a platform for debate and discussion. Justin eagerly welcomed the podium and launched into a defense of the Catholic faith. More or less with success, he turned out several works which we will look at. In return for his efforts, he was beheaded in about the year 165.

We have an interesting piece of work called *The Acts of St. Justin,* which are really the life of this saint and several others who died with him. In these works we find an account of Justin's discussion with the man who was eventually to sentence him to death. Justin makes it quite clear that as a believer he has a duty to spread the faith, and if the reward for such activity is death, then he is not only prepared but glad to accept it.

Justin's works that we have today are few but

important. The most important one is entitled *Dialogue with Trypho*. The book is an account of Justin's attempt to convert his friend Trypho. And it offers a world of Christian doctrine, images and arguments. Another of his writings (now lost) is a treatise entitled *Against Marcion*. This work takes on the Gnostics and others like them who with their own doctrines were perverting the thrust of Christianity. The first apology Justin addresses to none other than the emperor himself. Apparently, Justin was quite confident not only in his ability but in his credentials.

He addresses one letter to the Emperor Pius Antonius and another either to the same or to Emperor Marcus Aurelius and then launches into a long defense of the Catholic Church. The emperor, who had his own reputation as a philosopher and whose *Meditations* have come down to us in the popular form of the annual book sale of publishing houses, may or may not have received this apology. It is sometimes difficult to presume that any letter ever reaches its destination when addressed to a president, emperor or king. Nonetheless, the letter was boldly dashed off to the emperor, since he spoke at that time for all the world. Justin makes use of something that both he and the Romans had in common. Both enjoyed philosophy and both knew the classic sources. It was with this background that our apologist attempted to apply philosophy to the Christian message.

When we look at some of the contributions that Justin made to the world of theology, we find that he is among its first systematic thinkers. He very seriously attempted to coordinate the great currents of thought of his day with the faith. He took the theories of Plato and Plotinus and their preoccupation with images and intellectual abstractions and he applied them to Christ as the Word of God. In the area of man's own self-deceit, Justin labored to make the full force of revelation understood. The apologist knew that on his own man always invents false gods. Each generation has always made its own god to its own image. If one wants war, then man builds a theology of war. If one worships wealth, he constructs a theology of riches. If we are satisfied by lust, we fabricate a theology of permissiveness.

Against this approach to religion Justin attempted to introduce into the pagan intellectual world the idea of revelation. He also tried to convince his hearers that there was the possibility of an intervention by God into the daily life of that day. The heart and soul of Justin's apology can be seen in his constant effort to make the presence of God felt. God was not an invention. God lives. Christ was not a concept. Christ is a Savior. Into the world of Roman philosophy, law, order and wealth, Justin introduced a revealed God who spoke to men and demanded of them faith. The idea was as novel then as it is now — that God could be heard above the shouts and cries of man's own efforts.

There is a very interesting section in which Justin talks about immortality and the resurrection. Like St. Paul, he must have been laughed at at first, because these were not popular themes in a world that could not accept life after this life or the resurrection of a body.

In his letter to the emperor, Justin attempts to make commonsense his starting point. Marcus Aurelius belonged to the Antonine family. They were an illustrious and for the most part decent family. They gave to Rome some order and to the imperial throne a bit of integrity. It was for this reason, one assumes, that Justin felt that he had an eager listener in the person of the emperor. In any case, he goes on at great length trying to point out to his political leader the need for religion and religious principles in a highly complex and brutal world.

For us Justin remains an heroic figure. His field was apologetics. He was a teacher of the faith. His efforts bore fruit where the ground was receptive to the seed of his word. Like every believer Justin had the great dream of spreading his belief — his faith.

Cyprian

THE CHURCH IN AFRICA

Who then is so wicked and perfidious, so made with the fury of discord as to believe that the unity of God, the garment of the Lord, the Church of Christ, can be rent — as to dare to rent it?

—St. Cyprian
'The Unity of the Catholic Church' (No. 8)

As we move out of the second century of our era and into the third century, we come to St. Cyprian. The time was one of change and danger. The last of the Antonine emperors, Commodus, was assassinated in 193. As happened at the death of many emperors, the state fell into a period of anarchy. Everyone grabbed for power, and many people found their hands amputated in the struggle. An African by the name of Septimius Severus finally got control of the reins. With his ascension to the throne, Rome again breathed easily. The Church was even able to breathe deeply. Severus did not share Marcus Aurelius' intellectual antipathy for the Christians. In fact, there were Christians in his court. He had long since come into contact with various Eastern religions and he was open to a limited type of religious liberty.

Most probably Cyprian, whose full name was Thascius Caecilius Cyprian, was born at Carthage. He too was an African. The date of his birth is fixed by various authors as between 200 and 210 A.D. He was a citizen of a world that was totally Roman. Carthage in 146 B.C. had been utterly destroyed by the power of Rome. It had up until that point challenged Rome's authority and, more importantly, her trade routes in the Mediterranean. After its destruction, it became a Roman colony and was gradually integrated into the Empire. By the time Cyprian came on to the scene, centuries had passed, the city was again flourishing, and life had returned to all of North Africa.

Most of what we know about Cyprian we know from his writings, his treatises and the letters. We also know of his martyrdom through a short memoir of his life that was written by a deacon named Pontius. This work, one of the first Christian biographies to attain any type of popularity, is very valuable. Although it is not a finely polished work, it offers us a firsthand account of the life of a great man.

Cyprian's family was wealthy and well-educated. The young Cyprian, therefore, had all the benefits of a cultivated family background. As others before him, he too had the great desire to make his mark in the world of philosophers. It was in search of learning that he eventually came to the Church.

In his treatise *To Donatus* he tells us that God gave him the special grace of conversion by opening his mind to the truth. St. Jerome goes into more detail and tells us that he had come under the influence of an older priest, and, attracted by this man and his teachings, he eventually was baptized. According to Pontius, this took place on the eve of Easter in the year 246. Under the influence of the priest Jerome mentioned, Cyprian began to take seriously the counsels we find in the Gospels and eventually sold all his property, giving the return to the poor.

Cyprian was raised to the office and dignity of the priesthood almost immediately after his conversion, and he eventually came to be selected Bishop of Carthage. The traditional form of selecting the bishop in Carthage in the mid-third century was by a manner not clear to us today. But we do read that he was elected "by the voice of the people" over the opposition of some of the priests. Cyprian was already then known for his learning, piety and unbending devotion to the faith.

Hardly a year had gone by after his conversion when a new threat to the Church came from the imperial throne. In the person of the new emperor, Decius, the persecution of the Church entered a new phase. Decius was one of the many emperors that governed in the name of Rome during a sixty-five-year period of general chaos. The confusion began with the death of Emperor Caracalla in 217. This emperor had attempted to keep everyone happy by the simplest means — buying their support. An example of this is familiar to any tourist who visits Rome in the summer and attends the outdoor opera. Aida, Rigoletto and other spectaculars are presented in the ruins of the huge baths built by Caracalla. Now there is an admission fee. Then the baths were free to all.

A great favorite with the troops, Caracalla lavished on them huge sums of gold. He made the idea of an "imperial bonus" an institution. To calm the wealthy families, he widened the already cavernous tax loopholes. When this emperor died, the state was bankrupt. The Roman legions had been demoralized, and there was only a mere semblance of order in the civil administration and government structure. Coinage had been debased, trade was waning, inflation was raging, communications were faltering and murder was as much a commonplace as the sniffles.

In this climate no civilian government could work. The army spoke up. The result was confusion. The legions took turns at selecting emperors and then getting rid of them. Until Diocletian arrived to take on the purple robes of office in 284, a whole series of "emperors" came and went. A few reigned a couple of weeks. Some were plain thugs, others were degenerates, many never even saw Rome, and all died violently. Decius was one of these. He is chiefly remembered for his institution of the first general persecution of the Christians. Until then, persecutions had been sporadic and more or less dependent on the zeal of any given local governor or proconsul. Decius — failing to reorganize his own army, the state transportation system, or the tax structure, and afraid to tackle the enormous economic problems of the Empire — sought relief in a general attack on Christians. He made one very simple test the norm of life and death, freedom or imprisonment. One would have to offer worship to the "divine emperor." His edict, published in January of 250, provided the bishop be put to death and others were to be punished and tortured until they saw their way clear to renounce Christ. Immediately Pope Fabian in Rome was martyred. Cyprian fled Carthage, and the Church in Africa underwent a time of great confusion.

The majority of the Christians at Carthage apostatized, that is, they rejected the practice of the faith. Those who fell away from the Church were in two main groups: those who purchased a certificate that stated they had sacrificed to the emperor even when they had not. The certificate — like a party registration card — accorded the bearer instant "good standing." It was called in Latin *libellus*. The cardholders were naturally enough called *libellatici*. In the other group were those who really did fall away from the faith. These, after the Latin word for "fallen," were called *lapsi*. The *lapsi* had actually denied the faith but now in great part were repentant believers.

The problem eventually arose as to what to do with those who wanted back into the Church. One group of confessors was in favor of immediate reconciliation of any and all *lapsi*. They argued that under pressure, these people had fallen. The pressure was off. Therefore, they should be given a penance and forgiven.

Cyprian, on the other hand, felt that a more rigorous stand was needed. His position was that if in danger of death, the person be restored to communion with the Church; otherwise, he should wait until after the persecution had really ended. It was Cyprian's design to have a coundil in Rome and at Carthage to agree upon a common policy. This was the first time the Church faced the problem of apostasy and repentance on such a large scale, and so some common policy had to be worked out. The question was not a doctrinal one. The Church has

from the days of the New Testament admitted repentance — much like St. Peter's. But as the problem had
become widespread, Cyprian wanted to establish a
universal discipline, or at least a general procedure
with which to work.

As so often happens when a disagreement takes
place, events escalate. Those who opposed Cyprian in
the first place took the "I told you so" position. They
rallied in opposition to him and sent off to Rome to
complain. Cyprian in his turn, with a less than gentle
reply, excommunicated the group who refused his instruction.

Out of all the fighting that went on until Pope
Stephen settled the matter in Rome came two of Cyprian's works of great theological value. They reflect
the Church's understanding of what exactly is the
"local" Church. In the published works *The Lapsed*
and *The United Church,* a picture of the Church universal and yet local develops.

The universal Church is made up of many and
varied local churches. Granted, the one, holy, apostolic and catholic Church is more than just a federation of individual churches; it is, nonetheless, made
up of local churches throughout the world. These
local churches are essentially the same today as they
were in the days of Paul — the communities of believers centered in a specific area around one bishop,
their bond and symbol of unity in faith and charity. It
is true that there is but one Church, as but one baptism and one Lord, and that it extends over all the
world with its head, Peter, in Rome; but each local
church is also truly the Church. The local church is
the universal Church in miniature. Every local bishop, with his priests, preaches the same Gospel, dis-

penses the same healing grace through the sacraments, and applies to all the believers the saving mysteries of redemption. When the local bishop preaches, his church hears the words of the Church. When the local church prays, it prays as the Church. It is, therefore, not just a part of the Church; it is the Church — localized.

The universal Church, on the other hand, is more than the federation of local churches. It too is a reality extending over all the face of the world, giving that super-local dimension to the notion of the universal Church. Peter presides over the universal Church. The local bishop, successor of the Apostles, presides over the local church. Both are communities — one on a local level centered in the bishop, the other on a trans-local level centered in Peter, uniting all the local churches in one Church. The members of the local church by that title are members of the Church universal.

Each local church bears a relation to every local church in the universal Church. For every bishop is called to the succession of the body of Apostles known as the college of bishops. Each local bishop, therefore, has a relationship not only to his local church but to the Church universal. Each bishop by that title bears some responsibility for the whole Church.

In his earliest work after his conversion, *To Donatus,* Cyprian writes a strong exhortation to Christian living. In his treatise *The Dress of Virgins,* Cyprian presents a vigorous argument for the Christian counsel of virginity and the equally difficult virtue of chastity. Augustine refers to this work of Cyprian's in his own work *Christian Doctrine.* The influence of Cyprian's work is seen in the many references to it not only by Augustine but by Jerome and other leading figures in the life of the Church. St. Jerome found this work so formative as to recommend it to those virgins entrusted to his supervision. Augustine quotes the work of Cyprian and pays particular tribute to this man's command of Latin and his style and elegance. In *The Lord's Prayer,* Cyprian takes to instructing those soon to be baptized. Deferrari writes of this work:

"The Lord's Prayer is considered as an outstanding monument to Cyprian's genius, and also the best work on the subject in the long history of Christianity. Even after Cyprian himself and his other works were largely forgotten, it had wide circulation. When Hilary of Poitiers (middle of the fourth century) was writing his commentary on the Gospel of St. Matthew, he passed over the portion which contains the Lord's Prayer, on the ground that Cyprian had said all that was to be said about it. St. Augustine shows his great appreciation of it in his letter to Valerian. He notes that Cyprian anticipated the arguments of the Pelagians by 200 years."

To build up the flagging spirits of the Catholics at Carthage, Cyprian wrote the treatise *Mortality.* The date of this work is not certain. But the apparent need for the work is. The Christians were demoralized, the Church in Africa had been torn apart by this fight over the readmission of sinners. Later verbal attacks on the part of the pagans became violent. The plague was raging in that part of the Empire, and no one wanted to brave the contagion even to care for the sick, let alone bury the dead. At this point Cyprian rose to remind one and all in his and our generation that the essence of Christian charity is not its limitation, its circumspection, its appreciation of medical exigencies but rather its self-giving in a total and complete manner. At this point, too, Cyprian reminds his readers of the world view of believers that necessarily includes belief in the life to come. Developing this premise, Cyprian goes on to remind each of his readers that if one believes, then one spreads his belief. If one is convinced, then one acts to tell of his conviction.

The Catholic witness involves a whole world view. Part of that view is that the faith must be spread. The view of life which we call "Christ-directed" rests on the firm faith that Jesus Christ is risen and forms, insofar as we let Him, an active, constructive part of our daily lives. Since we await His coming both in our own lives and in the world, we live under His personal influence. Our "way" is based on His words and example. This way of life must be all-encompassing. And faith must seek first its realization in the individual believer, then throughout the world. The corollaries of this overall view of life are to be worked out in the social and cultural practices that make up our daily life.

Every believer is called to the same work that was Christ's. He came to make known the Father. With this knowledge, we start out to build a world that acknowledges the Fatherhood of one God and the brotherhood of all men. But the message is demanding. For as the Father sent the Son, so does He send us. "Be you as perfect as your heavenly Father" (Matthew 5:48). To the extent that he lives his faith, the believer participates in this aspect of Christ's Incarnation. By embodying in his life and action the faith he professes, the man of earth makes visible and active Christ in the world.

Initiation and conviction are the cornerstones of witness. The former implies comprehension; the latter, acceptance. If the first stage of witness, that of learning the faith, is permitted to become truncated, no amount of good will can gloss over the defect in the testimony. The Church has witnessed through her long life many examples of good will dissipated or ill-directed.

Martyrdom was the path that Cyprian himself was to choose. Following the timeworn diversion of pointing to defenseless scapegoats when overwhelmed by problems, Valerian, the emperor after Decius, signaled a renewed persecution. The emperor was under attack in the north by the German tribes, in England, in the east and around the Black Sea. Some diversion from the real problems was needed. Much like Hitler in pre-World War II Germany, Valerian was looking for a defenseless group on which to vent his frustration. Hitler had his Jewish people, Valerian his Catholics. In 251 Cyprian was arrested. His interrogation is still extant in the proconsular acts of Cathage. He was exiled. His biographer describes his final end. Cyprian came under the regulations of a new imperial decree. The edict stated that bishops, priests and deacons be put to death at once. Senators, knights and others of rank should lose their wealth, and if still reluctant should die, and officers of the civil service should become slaves. Cyprian was brought back from exile in September of 258 and beheaded outside the city limits. He was the first African bishop to become a martyr.

Origen

In order to understand things divine, the most important thing needed is prayer.

— Origen
'Letter to Gregory'

According to Ephraim, Origen wrote over 6,000 volumes. St. Jerome adds that this is more than the average person would normally read in a lifetime. To accomplish this prodigious literary undertaking, Origen employed a whole labor pool of secretaries. We are told that some wealthy patrons of his provided him with as many secretaries and notetakers as he could use. It was said that Julius Caesar used to dictate to three secretaries at once to keep abreast of his correspondence. Origen, we are told, dictated his work to seven. In this manner he turned out more books in his writing career than existed in the library of any of the Ivy League colleges at their founding.

Nor was his material just so many potboilers for the Sunday supplement. His works were theological and scriptural, appreciated, even if not always agreed with, by the leading Christian literary figures of his day.

Quasten tells us that the greater part of his literary output is devoted to the Bible, and for this reason, he might be called the founder of biblical science. He attempted for the first time in the Church's life to do a critical text of the Old Testament. The work was staggering. It is almost beyond comprehension when we consider that he had not the tools with which to work that are available today. Given this fact, it is hard to understand how he could have alone completed what he called "The Hexapla" (The Six-Fold Bible). This piece of scholarship alone would have merited him a place in the sun in the groves of the academe. In six columns — hence the name — Origen lined up the Hebrew texts and the best Greek versions of it word for word so as to provide in the end his own critical edition. There are few believers, including students of theology, who have ever even read the entire Old Testament, let alone attempted a study in depth of any one part of it. This makes us wonder all the more at Origen's ability, stamina, scholarship and self-discipline.

Probably on account of this last point — his self-drive and controlled discipline — Origen came to be known as "the man of steel." His personal habits were strict. He used every available moment at work, prayer, preaching or meditation. Eusebius, the historian, gives a clear account of the spiritual state of Origen. In speaking of his asceticism, he writes of Origen: "He preserved as far as possible the most philosophic manner of life, at one time disciplining himself by fasting, at another measuring out the time of sleep, which he was careful to take never on a couch, but on the floor. And above all, he considered that those sayings of the Lord in the Gospel ought to be kept which exhort us not to carry two coats nor to use shoes nor indeed to be worn out with thoughts about the future" (*Ecclesiastical History,* Book 6, No. 3). We learn from this source, also, that Origen in an excess of zeal emasculated himself. It appears that he took the Gospel text (Matthew 19:12) in a literal sense.

Silvano Cola writes, however, that the view of Origen as "the man of steel" touches only one aspect of this towering personality. If we concentrate just on his writings, we fail to see that behind the mountain of books, treatises and other writings, was a man, and a very holy man. Through his works shines the light of a spiritual man — a man of prayer. Again we refer to Cola, who sees Origen possessed of a "most delicate soul, blessed with tremendous natural and spiritual sensibility and above all else, a mystic." In his prayer life, we are told that he remained, in spite of his great store of knowledge, a child before God.

This man Origen, on whom so much praise and also reproof have been heaped, was born in Alexandria in Egypt. This city — founded by Alexander the Great in his march across Egypt — was a commanding port on the Mediterranean at the mouth of the Nile River. Even by the time Julius Caesar landed there, the city was renowned for its library and as an intellectual center. It was what might be called today a "university city." From our sources, it seems that Origen was born into a Christian family — the eldest son of a rather large family. His birthdate must have been somewhere around 185, because we know from his father's death in 202 that Origen was just a teen-ager. The martyrdom of Origen's father points out the already strong faith of the young Origen. After his father had been seized, tried and sentenced to death, Origen manifested a desire to share the lot of his father. Only his mother's quick action in hiding his clothes so he could not get out of the house seems to have kept the young Origen from an early death.

In his own words, Origen describes the pain and excitement of those days of his youth. "In those days, the faith was very much alive. It was a time in which martyrdom knocked at the door of everyone from the moment of his birth. It was a time in which those returning from the cemetery where they had just carried the bodies of their martyred friends and relatives gathered in church. Because this was a time when the Church was for them everything, I remember very, very well having seen in those days tremendous prodigies. The faithful were few, and they suffered greatly. But then again, those who remained faithful chose the straight and narrow path that leads to salvation" *(Homily on Jeremiah)*.

With the death of his father, the style of life of his family drastically changed. Origen was now the breadwinner. Their property was confiscated by the state, and to make ends meet, Origen became a teacher. Fortunately for the financial condition of his family, he was able to find work in the famous School of Catechumens at Alexandria. Fortunately for the Church, Origen in that post succeeded in revitalizing the school and attracting great numbers of young pupils. Eusebius says that the young were attracted to him not just by his words but by his very way of life. "As was his speech, so was the manner of life that he displayed, and as his manner of life, so his speech, and it was especially for this reason that with the co-operation of the divine power he brought so many to share his zeal" (*Ecclesiastical History*, Book 6, No. 3).

Apparently Origen would have been content to remain at the school at Alexandria. There he could teach, study and pray. But events proved otherwise. Certainly a man whose writing and fame had multiplied so much could not expect to remain hidden forever. And by the same token, having expressed so many opinions, Origen could not long remain without enemies. As often happens with the great, a cult grew up around him. Soon his works and words were being quoted in all types of contexts and to prove all species of arguments. The pain this caused him was great. In one section of his homilies on the Gospel of Luke, Origen refers to the exaggerations of his positions: "These exaggerations cause much suffering for me. Many that love me far beyond my merits are giving to my words and to the content of my teaching praise and meaning which they do not merit. Others, however, calumniate my writings, and they attribute to me opinions that I know I have never had. Everything they say about me seems to be false. One group says them out of love and the other out of hate" (*Homily on Luke*).

In addition to being thrown into the public arena of debate and argument, Origen soon found himself involved in an ecclesiological row. This unpleasant chapter began when Origen was forced to leave Alexandria. The Emperor Caligula in 215 looted the city of Alexandria. He closed its schools and persecuted its teachers. For this emperor, the intellectual life was very close to treason. Origen headed east for Palestine. Once there, he agreed to accept the invitation of the Bishops of Caesarea, Jerusalem and other Palestinian cities to give them some talks and to explain to the people there the words of Sacred Scripture. Origen was not a priest at this point. And when his own bishop heard of this, he was not exactly pleased. Demetrius, Origen's bishop, was upset. Origen — a layman — preached and presumed to teach Sacred Scripture to the faithful. According to Demetrius, this procedure was never heard of before. Origen was ordered home to Alexandria. He left immediately. However, to avoid this difficulty in the future — preaching the Word of God officially without ordination — the Bishop of Jerusalem ordained him. This move certainly did not calm Bishop Demetrius. It only made matters worse. Demetrius claimed he had to defend the present canon law which made it impossible for Origen, since he had mutilated himself, to be ordained. Eusebius tells us that the real reason for the flare-up was that Demetrius "was overcome by human weakness when he saw Origen prosper."

Whatever his motive, Demetrius called a gathering of the clergy at Alexandria, and here he reduced Origen to the lay state and then excommunicated him. Thus Origen entered a new phase in his life. He went again to Caesarea and opened a school of theology there. Apparently the bishops there paid little attention to the thunderbolts of Demetrius.

There has been much said and a great deal written about the "heresies" of Origen. Certainly there are points in his writings that diverge from the Church's orthodox and accepted position. But given the huge mass of his writings and the productivity of his genius it is not inconceivable that some errors should crop up. The sheer effort of singing all the great arias of all the great operas must induce even the most perfect singer to hit one sour note. So with Origen. We are told that he made the mistake of letting the philosophy of Plato influence his thinking. This led him on to very serious dogmatic errors. The most important of these was the doctrine of the preexistence of the human soul. The other difficulty in his style was his allegorical interpretation of Sacred Scripture. By interpreting the Word of God in terms of allegories, he, as Quasten points out, "introduced into exegesis a dangerous subjectivism leading to arbitrariness and error."

So deeply did the question of Origen's orthodoxy affect the Church that periodically there was a type of purge. These disputes came to be called the "Origenistic controversies." In them, nearly all of the theology and scriptural output of Origen was burned.

Origen was not the first teacher in the Church to make a mistake. He is not the last. In each age there are writers, teachers, preachers and exegetes who go off the track. Their works sell for a while — they obtain a certain notoriety. But hopefully in the end the error becomes evident and truth wins out.

What makes Origen an example today worth looking at is his firm determination to be and remain an orthodox and believing Christian. He never once compromised his intellectual demands, but he understood that any gift or talent for theology that he might have was to be always obedient to the Word of God and the voice of God's teaching Church. At the beginning of his chief theological work he writes, "That alone is to be accepted as truth which differs in no respect from ecclesiological and apostolic tradition" (*De Principiis,* Prol.). Origen understood that his theological witness had to be validated. All theological and exegetical witness must be authenticated.

Authentic witness must be related to the Church and identified with her mission because both share in the same witness of Christ. Theological witness is valid only in the context of the principal testimony given by the Church. The individual believer shares in the Church's ministry of testimony and office of witness only as he is in communion with her. This unity necessarily pertains to the doctrine taught and the faith handed down. As to the continuation of Christ's witness and the verification of the testimony concerning Christ Himself, the Church is the first and complete witness to God and the force of His mediation in the world today. The witness of an individual to the truth of the faith can never be independent of the witness of the Church for both speak of what they have — not of themselves — but of another.

When dealing with the faith, one testifies to something which is not his own in the sense that it is a communication of God's self-knowledge and His plan and not the position or opinion of any human. The witness to the faith relies not on one's own understanding of the revelation, but on the truth of God that gives it validity. "It is not ourselves we preach, but Christ Jesus," as St. Paul puts it. The message is beyond human understanding and is thus called supernatural. No human can, therefore, witness, the faith as he sees it divorced from the way it is presented as believed by the Church. Ultimately the witness is only valid insofar as it testifies to that which God has revealed and the Church proclaims.

Witness essentially relies on continuity between the fact witnessed and the testimony of it. Continuity is absolutely essential to authentic credible witness. And only in union with the Church can the individual find the continuity. His witness as it shares in the testimony of the Church can lay claim to the continuity of the living witness of the Church only as he is in communion and conformity with the faith as the Church believes and receives it. St. Paul in his first Epistle to the Corinthians argues the authenticity of his testimony in terms of what the Apostles believe and, therefore, its continuity with what the whole Church believes. In the Acts, to safeguard the testimony of the Church and insure its historicity and credibility, it was insisted that the number of Apostles, diminished by Judas' death, be filled only by "one of those who bore us company all the while we had the Lord Jesus with us, coming and going, from John's ministry of baptism until the day when He was taken from us — one of those must now join us as a witness to His Resurrection" (Acts 22). The individual witness participates in the witness that is the Church. He, therefore, shares in her continuity, and her infallibility, while he is joined to her as a witness. All the authenticity in his testimony depends on the relationship he maintains to that same Church.

For this reason Origen never intended to flout the Church's teaching office or reject her direction. Quasten tells us of Origen that "true, he committed errors — but no one can doubt that he always wanted to be an orthodox and believing Christian."

Broken by torture precisely to remain a believer under the persecutions of Decius, Origen died in 253 at the age of sixty-nine. He was buried in Palestine.

Eusebius

CHURCH REPORTER

The chief matters to be dealt with in this work are the following:

The lines of succession from the holy Apostles, and the periods that have elapsed from the Savior's time to our own. . . .

The names and dates of those who through a passion for innovation have wandered as far as possible from the truth. . . .

The widespread, bitter and recurrent campaigns launched by unbelievers against the divine message. . . .

The martyrdoms of later days down to our own time. . . .

—*Eusebius of Caesarea*
'The History of the Church'
(Book 1, No. 1)

So much of what we know about the early history of the Church depends on the *Ecclesiastical History* of Eusebius. From the Acts of the Apostles in the New

Testament on to the fourth century of the Christian era, the works of the early fathers are recorded. Eusebius therefore rightly can be called the father of Church history. And although he is not what we normally mean by the term "Church Father," he is certainly entitled to a place in any study of the writing of the early Church and its Fathers.

At first glance it seems that everybody in the fourth century was named Eusebius. Not a common name today, it was widespread at the time that the Emperor Constantine was unifying the flagging Empire of Rome by granting religious liberty to the Christians. At least forty famous contemporaries of our man bore the same name. Among these were two famous writers — Eusebius of Nicomedia and Eusebius of Samosarta. Since so many of these people figure into the history of the period, it is necessary to add an additional description — something like a last name — to keep them straight. Our Eusebius was bishop of Caesarea, and so when the problem arises he is designated as Eusebius of Caesarea.

Of his life we know very little. He was named bishop some time shortly after Constantine had granted religious liberty to the Catholics in the now-famous "Edict of Milan."

Most authors place Palestine as the land of Eusebius' birth and give the date as somewhere around 260 A.D. Caesarea might have been the city of his birth. This same city later saw him as the "first teacher of the faith."

At Caesarea was one of the flourishing schools of biblical study in the early Church. Caesarea rivaled Alexandria on the Egyptian coast for its learning and spiritual acumen. Here the theological tradition of

Origen was continued. To this school came Eusebius as a young man. Under the direction of a learned priest, Pamphilius, Eusebius attended class and soon became a friend of this first-rate scholar. Later, in tribute to the influence of his teacher, Eusebius incorporated into his own name that of Pamphilius. Eusebius wrote: "In the midst of all this glorious company shone forth the excellence of my lord Pamphilius, for it is not right that I should mention the name of that holy and blessed Pamphilius without naming him 'my lord' " (*Martyrs of Palestine,* Ch. 1).

The times in which Eusebius reached maturity were not peaceful ones for the Church. Paganism was again making one of its many "last stands" against the inroads of Christianity. Diocletian was emperor. His reign began in the year 284. For twenty-one years he ruled, and for a third of these years he directed a general persecution of the new faith. During this scourge, which continued under the Emperor Maxentius, Pamphilius was martyred in 310. This occasioned Eusebius' biography of his mentor, which earned Eusebius his first claim to fame as a writer.

Some time after the persecution ended around 313, Eusebius became Bishop of Caesarea. Here he remained as head of the Church for the next twenty-five years — the remainder of his earthly life.

The beginning of Eusebius' episcopal service witnessed the split of the forces of the Empire into two camps. One group favored the young Roman general, Licinius, the other the fledgling Emperor Constantine. The outcome of this struggle was to have immense impact on the Church. Licinius was not a believer. Constantine was. The two forces fought for control of the Roman Empire. To the support of Licinius came Maxentius, now noted mainly for his defeat at the Milvian Bridge near Rome. This event, usually accounted as responsible for Constantine's conversion, led to a reconciliation with Licinius and the proclamation at Milan of equal rights and freedom to all religions within the Empire. Later Licinius and Constantine came to another showdown at arms, and Licinius was defeated decisively. Henceforth, Constantine became sole ruler of the Roman Empire. His reign divides Roman history.

Eusebius writes on the history of the Church up to the reign of Constantine. Beginning with the works of Christ and His contemporaries, Eusebius shows the gradual growth of the Christian Church. His *Ecclesiastical History* is peppered with many facts of the early Christian life that might otherwise be lost to us. Particularly important is Eusebius' testimony on the growth of the Church in Rome. He describes the arrival of Peter in Rome "clad in divine armor like a noble captain of God. He brought the precious merchandise of the spiritual light from the East to those in the West, preaching the good news of light itself and the soul-saving word, the proclamation of the Kingdom of Salvation" (Book 2, 15).

The young Christian Church at Rome could not hear enough of what Peter had to say. They wished to conserve every memory of this man who had looked upon the face of the Lord. Eusebius describes how they persuaded Mark to write a summary of Peter's teaching. Peter's hearers, not satisfied with a single hearing or with the oral teaching of the divine message, resorted to appeals of every kind to induce Mark to leave a written summary. Nor did they let him go until they had persuaded him, and this became responsible for the writing of what is known as "the Gospel According to Mark."

Following the chronicle of the Acts of the Apostles, our historian describes the appeal of Paul to be judged in Rome and his eventual transportation to the Eternal City. Nero was now emperor. No one seems to have had a good word for him. Tertullian wrote: "He (Nero) treated everyone with savagery." Eusebius calls him "the monster of depravity." And so it came about that this much-hated, unstable man, brutal enough to kill his own brothers, mother and wife, was, in the words of Eusebius, led on to the murder of the Apostles. It is recorded that in his reign Paul was beheaded in Rome itself and that Peter was likewise crucified. Eusebius writes: "The record is confirmed by the fact that the cemeteries there are still called by the names Peter and Paul, and equally so by a churchman named Gaius who was living with the Bishop of Rome." Gaius has this to say about the places where the martyred remains of the two Apostles have been reverently laid: "I can point out the monuments of the victorious Apostles. If you will go as far as the Vatican or the Ostian Way, you will find the monuments of those who founded this Church."

That they were both martyred at the same time, Bishop Dionysius informs us in a letter written to the Romans: "In Italy they, Peter and Paul, died jointly in the same city and were martyred at the same time" (*Ecclesiastical History,* Book 2, No. 25). To the visitor of Rome today, the places of the burial of Peter and Paul are marked by churches. On the road to Ostia stands the Basilica of St. Paul Outside the Walls. At the Vatican, over what was once a pagan cemetery, stands the mighty dome of the Basilica of

St. Peter. Under that masterpiece of Michelangelo, in the recently excavated foundations, we can visit the final resting place of the bones of the fisherman from Galilee.

Eusebius provides us with one of the ancient lists of bishops to follow in the shoes of Peter. Like the old Roman canon, he begins with Linus. In successive pages he pieces together the whole first chapters of the life of Christian Rome. It is through Eusebius that we learn of the works of the bishops in Alexandria and Antioch and how these attempted to start centers of learning within their cities. Later, both these cities were to become the focal points of schools of theology which set the pace for religious thought for centuries.

It is from Eusebius that we learn of the long life and the activity of John the Apostle. Eusebius writes: "In Asia, moreover, there still remained alive the one whom Jesus loved, Apostle and Evangelist alike, John, who had directed the churches there since his return from exile on the island following Domitian's death" (Book 3, 21). Our historian offers us two other sources to bolster his opinion. He cites Irenaeus and Clement of Alexandria: That St. John survived so long is proved by the evidence of two witnesses who could hardly be doubted. Irenaeus writes: "All the clergy who in Asia came in contact with John, the Lord's disciple, testified that John taught the truth to them; for he remained with them until Trajan's time" (*Heresies Answered,* Book 2). Trajan became emperor in 98 A.D., and he ruled until 117 A.D.

Thanks to Eusebius, we also learn of many of the difficulties that hit the young Church. He provides us with a description of some of the first dissenters to the creed. Among those he describes are some who could not accept the divinity of Christ. We are told that they were willing to see Him as a fine, young, hard-working man who did much to call attention to the problems of the day. But they could not bring themselves to say that He was "the only-begotten Son of God." This Jesus of Nazareth was for them only a good man whose influence continues because of His strong personality and convictions.

Eusebius tells us of another group at odds with the true faith even from the earliest days. These people revered Jesus as a man upon whom the Holy Spirit had rested. He had undergone a baptism of the spirit but was not and should not be ever considered divine. For them, Christ remained a sort of dwelling-place of God. He was a good man in whom the Spirit of God lived and moved.

As a source book, *The History of the Church* at which we have been looking offers many valuable contributions to any study of the life of the early Christian community. From Eusebius we learn not only what was going on in the early Church but who was saying and writing what. His ten books approach being a "Who's Who" to the Christian world in its first 300 years.

From him we learn about the apostolic succession. He quotes where he can and picks up as many footnotes as possible to show his sources. Citing Irenaeus, he writes: "Having founded and built the Church, the Apostles entrusted the apostolic office to Linus. . . . Linus was followed by Cletus. After him in the third place from the Apostles the bishopric fell to Clement, who had seen the blessed Apostles and conversed with them and still had their preaching ringing in his ears and their authentic teaching before his eyes. . . . Clement was succeeded by Evarestus, and then Evarestus by Alexander; then Sixtus" (Book 5, 6). And so on goes the list until we are brought up to the end of the first century.

Much of Eusebius' work seems today to be almost a tale from another world. And perhaps by today's standards it is. He writes on bloody persecutions. His sixth book is almost entirely devoted to "widespread persecutions" under a series of emperors. He tells us of demoniac possessions, of ecclesiastical intrigues, of false doctrines taught in the name of Christ and of widespread confusion even in the ranks of Church leaders. Yet the permanent value of his work remains. Almost as a looking-glass into the past, Eusebius' *History* gives us a close-up of all that would now otherwise have been lost. Through his writings we are brought almost face-to-face with saints, frauds, bishops, persecutors of the faith and believers of the first centuries of the Church's life. For this alone we can be grateful. But our gratitude to Eusebius is not just that of a student to a teacher of past events.

His *History* also adds a note of balance to our preoccupations today. The Church has, as Eusebius points out, always suffered bad days. There always has been some confusion, some error, some false teaching. Certainly, her members have seen all this before. Unfortunately, some followers forget this sad fact. Of all of this Eusebius reminds the reader today. The history of the Church is a long one, with good days and bad — so it has been before, so it is now. For our efforts in coming close to the Church Fathers, we relied very heavily on Eusebius. He lived within earshot of these men, and the ink on their works was hardly dry before he was penning his own story of their lives and accomplishments. Eusebius therefore remains for us one of the first ports of call in any attempt to sail back into the days of the early Church.

With his *History* he has opened up to us not only the past and the ancient Church but has greatly aided us in the present by showing that things remain for each age pretty much the same. The same people who fill the pages of Eusebius' *History* walk the streets of our towns and cities. Their desires, their fears, their loves, their hatreds are all the same. Only some of the clothes, customs and manner of living differ.

Athanasius

FATHER IN EXILE

By His becoming man, the Savior was to accomplish two works of love: first, in putting away death from us and renewing us again; secondly, being unseen and invisible, in manifesting and making Himself known by His works to be the Word of the Father, and the King of the universe.

— St. Athanasius
'On the Incarnation' (No. 16)

South of Naples, on the quiet and sweeping Bay of Salerno, stands a monument to a Pope who died in exile. In the side chapel of the cathedral in this town, also noted as the point of the Allied landings in southern Italy during World War II, one finds a marble altar over the remains of Pope Gregory VII, better known as Hildebrand. On this altar is the simple inscription, "I loved justice and hated iniquity; therefore I die in exile."

Hildebrand, however, was not the first great exile for the faith. The rolls of the faithful include many a silent exile as well as those better known to history.

Athanasius is certainly one of the best-known exiles for Christ — for His Church and for the truth. And in the life of Athanasius we have a rare case of the vindication of a "martyr" before his death.

Athanasius enters into history at the critical moment of the Arian heresy. Arius, a priest of Alexandria, denied that Christ was God. His argument ran thus: There is only one God. He is eternal and completely self-sufficient. The Son of God, therefore, must be a created thing — a creature. Hence He cannot be God. Neither the Son nor the Holy Spirit possess the same being or substance as the Father. Arius put his finger on the very core of the question of the Trinity. How can God be one and three?

The theological question of how this could be was now to divide the Church. Some would follow one school of thought, others another, until finally the faith was in shreds and the whole fabric of the Church ripped asunder.

The matter was not one to be decided in the salons of the wealthy, over a drink with a university professor, or in the calm of a classroom. The question touched men's lives too intimately. Either Christ was God or He wasn't. This was the question that the faithful understood — the vast majority of the people. If He wasn't, then His death merited nothing and men were right back where they started out — back with Adam. If, however, as the Church has always held, Christ was God, then His death was a salvific one, as says St. Paul. "But when the fullness of time came, God sent His Son, born of a woman . . . that He might redeem those who were under the law, that we might receive the adoption of sons" (Galatians 4:4).

His sacrifice, as described by the author of the Letters to the Hebrews, was that of the divine Mediator between God and man. This Arius could not understand and did not accept.

The fight got started in Alexandria. It spread like a brush fire, and soon the whole edifice of the Church was in flames. The Emperor Constantine decided that the time had come to put some order into the spreading confusion. He convoked the first general Council of the Church. This was held in Nicaea in 325.

Already by this fact we can see what changes were taking place in the simple Church founded on the shores of the Sea of Galilee. The early Church, the ancient Christian community, found its leaders fully occupied in the task of spreading the Good News. Christ's Resurrection and Redemption was the message they carried. It knew neither geographical nor political bounds. In such fever and seeming disinterest in political structures, Paul could even seemingly pass over the institution of slavery while preaching Christ to both slave and freeman (Philemon 11:20). The only tools these disciples of Christ had were faith, zeal and enormous love. Neither force nor public office was acceptable in spreading the Gospel.

Within a few centuries, the inevitable happened. The Church prospered. Princes were baptized. Soon the sanctuary was crowded with political powers. Gradually what was a Gospel that spread because of men's example became an institutional part of a political system. So strongly did the emperors play their hand in Church affairs that by the great Council of Chalcedon in 451, the emperor named who would preside at the Council. Such procedures tempted Pope St. Leo's now immortal remark, referring to such political intrigues, that they were "not so much Councils as a get-together of bandits."

At the Council of Nicaea, Athanasius appeared with his bishop, Alexander. The matter of Christ's divinity was discussed, studied, prayed over and again confirmed as the teaching of the Church. It was not just a teaching of the Church which one could take or leave. It was an essential part of everything Christianity stood for — the reconciliation of man with God and men with men. Out of that Council came the creed which is so familiar to us today. It forms to our time a part of the Sunday liturgy and adds to the solemnity of the Mass of other feast days. Within this Creed — the Nicene Creed — the divinity of Christ is confirmed in such a way that it cannot be denied, at least within the Church.

However, the theological conclusions and political positions of many churchmen of this period did not readily welcome the Creed. Teachers, bishops and influential political leaders continued to see the doctrine as unnecessary or just plain false. So rapidly did the confusion and the rejection grow that St. Jerome lamented that one day the whole world would groan to find to its surprise that it was Arian.

Against this tide — the powerful tide of a raging storm — stood Athanasius, alone. He refused to accept the new doctrine preached by the followers of Arius. And perhaps more to his credit, he refused to accept the new mingling of religious office and civil political administration. He waged a lonely war.

When Constantine in 333 sought to rehabilitate Arius, Athanasius refused to accept him and his doctrine. Something had to give. The emperor for political purposes wanted Arius restored. Peace at any cost. Anything to keep his bickering bishops quiet. Athanasius alone said no. No new doctrines, no new denials of old doctrines and no new deals to redress old faults. Thus began the history of Athanasius' exiles.

He left Alexandria, where he had been consecrated bishop in 328. This was the first of five such exiles, the last three of which were spent in the solitude of the Egyptian desert. Cola writes that of his forty-five years as a bishop, Athanasius spent seventeen in exile, and these various exiles were for the most part spent with monks in the desert areas outside Alexandria. So disgraced was he at times that he was forced to hide himself in the tomb of his father.

The exiles visited upon Athanasius were the result of the long fight within the Church and the Empire over the meaning of what Nicaea taught. For Athanasius this doctrine was simple: it says Christ is the Son of God — of the same being as His heavenly Father — equal to Him from all eternity. However, the theological confusion and the political division so fogged up the scene that peace was not to come to the Church until years later. In the meantime, almost with a precision clocklike regularity, Athanasius was deposed from his bishop's office, exiled, recalled and rehabilitated. First under Constantine in 335, then under Constantius in 339, and again in 356, later under Julian in 362 and finally under Valens in 365. And almost as if by an irony of Providence, Athanasius returned for the last time to his see city under the Emperor Valens. All the trouble for Athanasius began under Constantine and his attempt to blend

Church and State. And our saint lived to see the entire Constantinian line perish. The last to go, Julian, was reported killed by his own troops. Thus ended the dynasty of Constantine.

St. Athanasius was essentially a witness. His life was one of continuing testimony to the faith and to that faith as explained within the Church. As such, Athanasius realized the importance of the continuity of his message with that of the Apostles and the need that all witness, lay and priestly, had within the larger witness of the Church.

The norm of one's judgment concerning the faith is to be that faith handed down to and through the body of believers from the Apostles. Paul is speaking to all the believers and of their faith as that believed, when he reminds the Romans of the norm of their faith and its relation to the whole Church (Romans 12:3). In the flesh this norm was Christ Jesus. In the world it is now the Church. The norm for adherence to both, one as the extension of the other, is the faith as believed by the Church. This touchstone is the exact same one used in the Old Testament to verify a true prophet. Does his message conform to the Word of God handed down and confirmed in the belief of the community? The message in the Old-Testament prophets, "Remain faithful to the belief of your fathers," recalls the prophets' incorporation of this criterion within their own witness.

St. Paul in his first Epistle to the Corinthians argues the authenticity of his testimony in terms of what the Apostles believe and, therefore, its continuity with what the whole Church believes. In the Acts, to safeguard the testimony of the Church and insure its historicity and credibility, it was insisted that the number of Apostles, diminished by Judas' death, be filled only by "one of those who bore us company all the while we had the Lord Jesus with us, coming and going, from John's ministry of baptism until the day when He was taken from us — one of those must now join us as a witness to His Resurrection" (Acts 22). The individual witness participates in the witness that is the Church. He, therefore, shares in her continuity, and her infallibility, while he is joined to her as a witness. All the authenticity in his testimony depends on the relationship he maintains to that same Church. For as the witness to Christ and God's mighty works, the Church is the first and only witness. All individuals share in this work as members of the Church and are to be always humble before her witness.

To the teaching Church is entrusted the obligation of spreading the faith, of passing on the saving word. She must bear witness to the presence of God and our life in Him. If man is to be saved by his participation in the saving action of Christ, if he is to be counted as one who "knows Christ" so that everyone who has faith in Him may possess eternal life, then he must know of that supernatural reality that is Christ and His redemptive plan. Each one must be given an opportunity to hear of that truth, to have it witnessed before him to have its reality testified in his presence.

In his fight with half the leadership of the Church, Athanasius also made another point. The Church can and does with divine authority state the faith even in words that are not necessarily found in the pages of Sacred Scripture. The Greek word *homoousion* caused many, including Athanasius and company, much trouble. Nicaea used it to establish a

70

touchstone that would state clearly the Catholic faith. It is a word that was impossible to square with any kind of Arian doctrine. Quite simply it means that Jesus and the Father are of the same stuff — the same substance, being, reality. Neither is superior to the other. For Athanasius, the living, conscious teaching Church is the guardian of both the message and its very wording. Christ's Church not only must pass on the saving Gospel, but can at times even indicate which words best serve the Gospel. The witness of the Church is not a vague hope or groundless euphoria. It is a clear testimony of precise events, a judgment articulated about certain facts. And as any society the Church has those called out of it to speak for it.

Obviously, the Church, as an organic whole, cannot testify. Her spokesmen do. Within the Church some are called to be the official and authentic spokesmen or witness for her. These called out of the Church, by the Spirit, for the Church, are those teachers, successors to the Apostles, called bishops. Of their functions in the Church, one primary duty is that of official witness or spokesman for the incarnate witness that is the living Church. The bishop for the local church and all the bishops for the universal Church, always with Peter as their head, bear the ministry of witness in a particular manner.

Athanasius' problems did not die with the death of Constantine in 337. In fact, under the rule of Constantine's son, Constantius, the situation turned from bad to worse. He again took up exile. The persecution continued under the short-lived reign of Julian the Apostate, so-called because he not only left the practice of the faith but attempted to revive paganism as a viable substitute for the Christian religion.

However, all these things passed away, and eventually Athanasius was returned for the last time to his see city, Alexandria. There, in the declining days of his life, he was able to look back over the turbulent years that had plagued him with the satisfaction that he had fought the good fight and had fought it well. He died at the age of 78 on May 2, 373.

Basil the Great

FATHER OF THE RELIGIOUS LIFE

If the man of God must be perfect, it is all-important that he be made perfect through the observance of every commandment "unto the measure of the age of the fullness of Christ"; for according to divine law, an offering that is mutilated, even if it be pure, is unacceptable as a sacrifice to God.

—*St. Basil*
'The Long Rules' (Preface)

Caesarea, the provincial capital of Cappadocia in Asia Minor, has produced its share of names known to the early Christian world. Unfortunately, the city no longer is part of that tradition, but its saints continue to exert enormous influence on the whole Church down to our own day.

Of these saints, Basil is an outstanding example. He is not, however, the sole or exceptional case of piety in an otherwise mediocre world. That land was fertile ground for many a saint. In fact, Basil was part of a family of saints. He shares the heavenly limelight

73

with his brother, Gregory of Nyssa, and a younger brother, St. Peter, as well as his sister, St. Macrina. Following the lead of his parents, Basil the elder, and his mother, Emilia, who were also saints, Basil had a head start on many of the Christians in his neighborhood.

In the early part of the second quarter of the fourth century, our Basil was born. He had the advantage of a good family and a comfortable childhood. This provided him a background from which he would later move on to difficult tasks with considerable ease. His father had prospered as a lawyer. In fact, his office was continually deluged with requests that he take this case or that one. The midnight oil burned late many a night in the office, and from his father, Basil also learned, besides piety, diligence and a great deal of self-discipline. As a father, the older Basil was determined to see that his children, too, were well-educated. The spiritual side of their training — the day-to-day formation in the world of spiritual values — he left to his wife Emilia. However, in the case first of Basil and then of his other sons — from a total family of ten — the more formal education was conducted at the great centers of learning of that day.

Basil was soon shipped off to Constantinople and then Athens, where he studied philosophy, rhetoric and mathematics. And in these cheerful student days he made as friends Gregory of Nazianzen, who was to become a lifelong close friend, and Julian, later emperor and apostate. The days passed quickly for the young man, and Basil soon found that he had exhausted what the schools had to give. He returned to Caesarea. It is in this period immediately after his return from school that Basil underwent a spiritual conversion.

He had, to be sure, been a devout youth. Aside from those pranks and diversions that are the right of all students, Basil was in no serious difficulty at school. In fact, in his school days he practiced a piety that certainly did justice to his upbringing. But at this particular time Basil seemed to have been called in a very special way by God. He says that he felt moved by the Spirit. It was at this time that he began to see that he was being asked to make a special commitment. He felt that he must in some way make a special reply to this motion of grace within him. Later he was to remark that the first fruit of any giving on the part of the Spirit should be a renewal of a man's faith in God (*Concerning Baptism,* Q. 8). The two go hand in hand. Sacred Scripture shows us that all the wonders and miracles worked by Christ had no other as their principal purpose than to bring forth faith. St. Paul reminds us that only in faith can we know the Spirit, and only in the Spirit can we call Christ Lord (Romans 8:15). If it is truly a renewal that God wills and that the Spirit urges, then the same Spirit must be breathing into the heart of man the grace necessary to confirm him in the faith.

Following on the faith must be the wish to share it. The most obvious sign (apart from their own personal faith) that the Apostles were quickened by the Holy Spirit, was their zeal to spread the faith. Once they realized what had been given them, they thought only of sharing it, and this explains what seems like St. Paul's almost frantic effort to reach so many parts of the Roman world within his short life-span.

Taken by the Gospel's call to witness, Basil

began an effort that would take up the greater part of his remaining life. He decided to form a community or to establish some sort of community life that would put into vivid practice the Gospel counsels of poverty, chastity and obedience. In this way he hoped to give the world a living witness to the validity of the Gospels. Eventually, as the idea caught on and more people gathered to join his monastery and follow his style, Basil was forced to establish a Rule that would provide an outline of spiritual practices and values. This was mainly intended to offer guidance to those who wished to take up a community form of life. As a result of both his Rule and its influence, Basil is considered in the Eastern Church what Benedict is to the Western — the father of monasticism.

Basil's Rule was aimed at the production of the devout life. He writes in the preface of his famous *Long Rules*, "Let us who are striving to live the devout life, who value the life of retirement and freedom from worldly distractions as an aid to the observations of evangelical doctrine" take up His laws and this Rule.

Basil notes how only love of God is really a worthy motive for any type of complete Christian living. He writes in one section: "To sum up, I note the following three kinds of disposition which necessarily compel our obedience: we avoid evil through fear of punishment and take the attitude of a slave; or, seeking to obtain the reward, we observe the commandments for our own advantage and in this we are like hirelings; or else, . . . out of love for Him who gave us the law, we rejoice to be deemed worthy to serve a God so good and so glorious and we are thus in the dispositions of sons" (*Long Rules*, Preface).

His famous Rule provided for a living away from the virtue-choking course of this life. It was to try to transport his followers into the realm of the Spirit. But Basil was aware at the same time that the Christian life is not a life turned solely towards another world. All believers are part of this world; our roots are here. Our love, our dedication to Christ must somehow overflow to reach all men here and now. Christian community must be built up — or at least begun now — so that some day it can be perfected. However, this perfection if it is to be done in a religious community must model itself more completely on the Gospels. The Gospel, in describing God's eternal, divine, immense love, saw it as one that loved the world unto the death of His own Son. So, the Gospel notes, every religious must somehow turn outward to the world to make it see the love that is God.

The first effect of the love of God that is the driving force of one who has chosen a religious life ought to be an uncompromising fraternal charity (*Long Rules*, Q. 3). More than any other Christian, the religious must recognize the love of God in the love of our fellowmen. Here we touch on one of the great services of the Christian community that religious life offers. Within the Church, which is itself a sign, the religious is a sign. That life must point out to others the love, understanding, compassion and truth of Christ. This type of religious life is a sign within the great sacramental sign which is the Church. By being a light, the monk, nun or religious brightens the way for others within the Church and thus offers her greatest service to the Christian community.

It is in the light of our long, slow, stumbling

march to another, more perfect home that the religious life makes sense. Knowing that we have a destination, a life beyond this life, the religious can gladly offer himself as a sign that points the way. Only in this context as Basil describes it can mortification or self-disciplinary programs make sense *(An Ascetical Discourse)*. As a spiritual person, the religious is and must remember that he is a visible marker on a rough road to an invisible Kingdom. By his visibly dedicated life he shows all men that God has already begun his final work on earth and that this divine labor will be capped in glory in the life to come. Those who offer this in religious life are a living sign which can and ought to attract all the members of the Church to an effective and prompt fulfillment of their own Christian vocation.

Because of this privileged witness, the religious has a special work in the Church. As a spiritual person, he reaches out to God to enrich his own personal relationship with Him while he walks with men to show Christ in His work and life for others. In doing so, the religious becomes a visible, a very visible, effective sign. The Church greatly needed this two-way street at the time of Basil, and it needs it today. Without this concrete sign there would be a danger that the charity which animates the Church would grow cold and the paradox of the Gospel would be blunted.

This double action of spiritual work is the work of religious. They are to know God and make Him known. Their lives are not just private preserves of easy prayer, but a constant powerful activity that has as its goal to spread the Gospel. To follow only one direction of this two-way street, a road that leads to the Father and to men, is to turn religion and religious life into a constant self-preoccupation or, even worse, into a privileged camp of self-concern. The Rule of Basil takes constant note of this danger and directs much of the energy of his followers into a true dedicated self-giving. In terms of the great needs of the Church for real witness to the Gospel, the religious cannot afford to turn in on himself. He must offer the world something. That something is a witness to the faith and a love of the Church in and for Christ.

Along with all of the great founders of religious orders, from the first hermits in the Egyptian desert on through the latter-day founders of active communities in Western Europe, Basil knew that the religious commitment is clear and possible only to a man of faith. The total commitment of one's self, one's life, energies, love and talents to a life of discipline, community work is unintelligible and impossible without the eyes of faith. St. Paul reminds us that to the world we seem foolish, we *have* to seem foolish. Only with the eyes of faith, faith that Jesus is risen and is with us and will come again in glory, only with these eyes can we see the "why" of religious faith. By incorporating into his Rule the place of evangelic counsels, Basil provided for a genuine witness to that and also portrayed a world apart in which God's "new creature" could flourish (*Long Rules,* Q. 2).

Each religious who takes up Christ's call to follow Him says, with all his life and energy, that we — all of us — already belong to another Kingdom. He says with the quietness of a vow that we are attempting to become, in the words of St. Paul, "an altogether new creature" (Galatians 6:17). He says there are other options available; that life need not burn itself out in a handful of years. He knows that chastity for the Kingdom's sake frees man's heart and becomes a special source of spiritual richness in the world, a spiritual richness for which the world is parched.

Yet the "new creature" of St. Paul requires a "new creation." Personal holiness is part of the holiness of the whole Christian community. With this in mind, the work of a religious must be turned not solely toward one religious community, as if it were an incarnation of the whole Church, but toward the good of the whole Church, and through the Church, to all men. The "new creation" demands justice, truth, love and all the beauty of the Gospel. But it cannot be built through acts of self-gratification or self-concentration. It is the result of the work of all the Christian community working together, confident that we can build a "new world."

Using the question-and-answer technique in his *Long Rules,* Basil confronts us with the problematic that necessarily comes with an attempt at community living.

But you may say: Can't this be done without community life, without obedience? Can't I do it on my own? Of course, you not only can but must seek to spread the knowledge of Christ — as a disciple. We all must. Every believer is called to be a witness to all that Christ did and said. To the extent that he lives his faith, the believer participates in the work that was Christ's. By embodying in his life and action the faith he professes, the man of this life makes Christ visible and active in the world. Of this there is no question! This is what Christian witness is all about.

This is what happens in all those areas of daily concern — politics, medicine, engineering, labor, economics, law — when a dedicated Christian lives his faith (*Long Rules,* Q. 9).

But the contribution of the religious to the Church and world order is not confined just to this type of witness. The genius of the religious commitment is its totality — a luxury not permitted those who must raise a family and meet a mortgage payment. It gives of self completely without reserve. There are no prior commitments or previous obligations. It is a completely free, completely whole self-giving. The uniqueness of religious witness is in its capability "of accepting the abnegation of poverty, and of being attracted by simplicity and humility; it is that of those who love peace, who are free from compromise and set on complete self-denial — of those who are at the same time free and obedient, spontaneous and tenacious, meek and strong in the certainty of the faith."

Unfortunately for his little flock of followers, Basil was not destined to remain in the quiet of his newly formed spiritual city. Other duties were soon imposed on him. He was ordained, and his old friend Gregory Nazianzen called to him for help in defense of the true faith against the inroads of Arius. As things fell out, Basil eventually became Bishop of Caesarea. And in this most influential post, he established his reputation for a strong defense of the faith. The same post also brought him into direct political contact with the Emperor Valens.

Valens was an Arian. He was also a politician. And so much as he wished to be rid of Basil, he could not budge him. Even a show of royal force did not frighten Basil. And Valens could not, or, perhaps better said, dared not arrest him. Basil's strength, which had gradually grown over his increasing years as a bishop, came from the people. They admired him, they looked to him for guidance, and they considered him a holy man. They were not altogether sure of the motives that their emperor had for disliking their bishop, but they were certain that they liked the bishop and on whose side they were to be found in any showdown. Another element also gave the emperor a second thought. Basil's recently formed religious communities were spreading, and spreading fast. And with them came a new aspect of the organized Church. Where before there was nothing, the new monasteries and convents, with their monks and nuns, were offering schools, orphanages, medical clinics and putting the charity of Christ into practice. To attack this, when all his civil administrators offered was increased taxes, was more than even Valens could do openly.

Peace, however, did not follow. The bishops who chose the political support of Valens and who still shared the political doctrine launched an underground war against Basil. Political and ecclesiastical technicalities were harped upon. By misunderstanding, half truth and false representation, Basil found himself being charged with heresy. He describes the world into which he was thrown after he left his religious foundation. In writing to his monks in December of 375, he says: "At the same time, the difficulty of this present critical situation, in which all churches have been shaken and all souls are sifted, causes us much anxiety. For some have opened their mouths unsparingly against their fellow-servants.

Falsehood is fearlessly spoken; the truth is completely veiled. The accused are condemned without trial; the accusers are believed without examination. For this reason, although I heard that many letters are being circulated against me, marking and denouncing us and bringing accusations about affairs for which we have a defense ready, I decided to keep silent, and I did."

His plight took a turn for the good only when Valens was fatally wounded in the battle of Adrianople in 378. The pressure was temporarily off Basil. But broken in health and worn out with self-discipline and selfless work, he died in 397 on the first day of the year. He left behind a legacy of monastic life, of institutionalized charity and a working Rule for a devout life.

The Two Gregorys

FATHERS AGAINST ARIUS

What is this new mystery concerning me? I am small and great, lowly and exalted, mortal and immortal, earthly and heavenly. I am connected with the world below, and likewise with the spirit. I must be buried with Christ, rise with Christ, be joint heir with Christ, become the Son of God, even God Himself.

—St. Gregory Nazianzen
'On His Brother, St. Caesarius'

The Council of Nicaea opened in 325. It was the first of the general ecumenical Councils of the Church. In just a little more than a hundred and twenty-five years the Fourth Council — that of Chalcedon — was held. Within the framework of these two Councils, so much history of Catholic belief and Christian theological history is packed that no one can seriously study the doctrine of the Church without concentrating on this era. This was the "long century" out of which came the Church's definitive statements on the

Trinity, Christ's divinity, His nature, the divinity of the Holy Spirit, and the role of Mary in man's redemption. Newman writes that "it is impossible to view historical Christianity apart from the doctrine of the Trinity." And if we want to see how that doctrine came to clarity, we must turn to the "long century" — from Nicaea to Chalcedon.

This was also the long century of Church Fathers. Across its years and in and out of many Councils and discussions and books came such Fathers as Athanasius, Basil the Great, Gregory Nazianzen and Gregory of Nyssa. But the great century of Christian theology did not begin with one of the Church Fathers. It started with a mistake.

The matter that brought the 300 bishops to Nicaea in 325 was a new theology and a new theologian. The new theologian was Arius of Alexandria, and his new theology is described by Newman. "It was the doctrine of Arianism that our Lord was a pure creature, made out of nothing, liable to fall, the Son of God by adoption, not by nature, and called God in Scripture, not as being really such, but only in name. At the same time [Arius] would not have denied that the Son and the Holy Ghost were creatures transcendently near to God, and immeasurably distant from the rest of creation."

Arius had not intended to introduce into the serious halls of theological studies a question about an interpretation of Sacred Scriptures. Or if he did, he proceeded in a way that could be described by later students of history as a "Madison Avenue" approach to the selling of his new theology. Employing sermons, handbills, pamphlets, books, popular hymns, liturgical rallies and catchy songs, Arius set out to "teach" the faithful his view of Christ. The picture of Jesus — the somehow created wonder-worker, good guy — came across like a shock wave. It was the latest thing. It was fresh. It was new — and it was false.

Again Newman tells us that Arius' doctrine contradicted everything held on the Trinity by the Church up to the day his class notes began being passed about. He writes: "There was during the second and third centuries a profession and teaching concerning the Holy Trinity, not vague and cloudy, but of a certain determinate character, and this teaching was 'contradictory and destructive of the Arian hypothesis.' And from all this literature the fact emerges that, from the beginning, 'some doctrine or other of a Trinity lies at the very root of the Christian conception of the Supreme Being, and of his worship and service': and that 'it is impossible to view historical Christianity apart from the doctrine of the Trinity.' "

Arius himself writes of his own position. In a letter to Eusebius of Nicomedia, Arius writes: "What is it that we say, and think, and have taught, and teach? That the Son is not unbegotten, nor a part of the unbegotten in any way, nor [formed out] of any substratum, but that he was constituted by [God's] will and counsel, before times and before ages, full (of grace and truth), divine, unique, unchangeable. And before he was begotten or created or ordained or founded, he was not. For he was not unbegotten. We are persecuted because we say, 'The Son has a beginning, but God is without beginning.' For this we are persecuted, and because we say, 'He is [made] out of things that were not.' But this is what we say, since he is neither a part of God nor formed out of any sub-stratum."

The fight between Arius and the Church authorities began about 323. Then theological discussion of points that important resulted in great public interest. Even without mass media, word spread and conflicting ideas circulated. By 325 the situation was out of hand. Riots now accompanied discussions; and among the bishops some were confused, some were frantic, but all were deeply concerned about what was happening to the Church of Christ.

The matter had also become one of public order. And in those days, events of such import soon reached the emperor's desk. His reaction was swift. He issued a call for the bishops of the Empire to come together to settle the matter — once and for all. Today it seems shocking that the leading political figure would call a Church council. With our centuries of experience — good and bad — behind us, and our various forms of Church-State separation policies, as well as enormous apathy regarding religion, the action of Constantine seems startling. Then it was natural. He spoke for all civil government. He was personally responsible for the entire Empire — its affairs and its order. And there was no other pole. The Empire was all the European world knew, and the emperor was all that the Empire recognized. We almost have to step back slowly 1,600 years to understand what was the setting of those days that produced the second generation of Church Fathers and the "long century" of theological debate.

Constantine was sole ruler of the then known world. His title, "Augustus," was sacred. One knelt in his presence, and one kissed the sacred purple that clothed him. The Empire with its seat on the Bosporus at the new city of Constantinople included — besides Italy — all of Europe west of the Rhine and south of the Danube, Britain, all of what is now Turkey, the Middle East, Egypt and all of North Africa to the Atlantic. And in every major city in each province of the Empire, the Church was making headway, converting, teaching, preaching and becoming a part of the scene. If then she — the Church — were to be divided in doctrine, the Empire would be seriously affected. If the Church were to suffer a nervous or intellectual breakdown, it would not be long before the same symptoms would affect the body politic. This the emperor could not let happen.

And so the Council met — with no precedents, no rule books, no past procedures to guide it. It met to tackle one problem, and it created its own rules as it did so.

Nicaea is about sixty-five miles from Constantinople on the Bosporus. It was then about twenty-five miles from the temporary imperial captial, Nicomedia. We can gather some idea of the imperial splendor when we stop to think that this place was chosen because it could accommodate 300 guests easily. It was the emperor's summer palace. The gathering came together on May 20. Hughes thus described the body of bishops: ". . . The vast bulk of them (were) from the Greek-speaking lands where the trouble was raging, Egypt, Palestine, Syria and Asia Minor. But there were bishops also from Persia and the Caucasus, from the lands between the Danube and the Aegean, and from Greece. There was one from Africa and one from Spain, one from Gaul and one from Italy, and since the great age of the Bishop of Rome forbade his making the journey he was represented by two of his priests."

The two priests sent by the Pope presided over the meeting. Even with no past program to direct its procedures, it appears that the bishops understood immediately that for the Council to be an ecumenical one it was necessary that the Pope be present at least through his representatives or explicit approval.

Arius lost. The traditional faith won. This is the final scorecard of the Council. The Creed affirmed that Christ was and is "of the substance of the Father." Thus the Church entered into the "long century" of fighting to get this doctrine accepted by those who had backed Arius.

Onto this stage came some of the most interesting Fathers of the liturgical calendar. Butler tells us that "in view of his resolute defence of the truths promulgated by the Council of Nicaea, St. Gregory Nazianzen has been declared a doctor of the Church and has also been surnamed 'the Theologian' — a title which he shares with the Apostle St. John."

But Gregory of Nazianzen was not the only Gregory of the era to enjoy a title. St. Gregory of Nyssa was called by the Second Council of Nicaea the "Father of the Fathers." He is also called "the column supporting the whole Church."

These two Gregorys form an integral part of the history of the "long century." Gregory of Nyssa, so called because he was later to be the Bishop of Nyssa, was the brother of St. Basil and shared in all that that holy and illustrious family had to offer.

Gregory of Nyssa's writings are considerable. They include works on Sacred Scripture, mystical and ascetical studies, catechetical exhortations and dogmatic theology. Perhaps one of the most interesting and relevant to our day is Gregory's *Address on Religious Instruction,* which is sometimes called the "Catechetical Oration." Basically, this work is a compendium of Christian doctrine. And it cannot but be of great interest to the Church in the twentieth century to look back at this fourth-century catechism to see in it what this Church Father considered essential Christian doctrine. Gregory had in mind as he wrote this "handbook" — this teacher's guide — a catechism that would give an overall view of the faith to those of the laity as well as ordained priests who were teaching the faith.

Some of these had organized classes in a more formal style, many relied on gatherings in the homes of believers, a few had even set up real schools — all to teach the faith. These teachers were called catechists. And to make their work easier, Gregory turned out his "teacher's guide." Although Gregory uses the prevalent Greek philosophy as a means to explain the faith, his primary starting point is the teaching of the Church. The authors of *Christology of the Later Fathers* note of Gregory's catechetical effort: "There can be no doubt, however, that this Address gives, in its relatively small compass, a remarkable survey of Christian doctrine and reflects the genius of Eastern theology at its best. The teaching of the Church is adapted to the Hellenic environment and made intelligible to the Greek.

"Gregory's Address appears to have been widely circulated in the Eastern Church, and to have influenced later writers."

Of particular beauty and skill is the section on the Eucharist. Here Gregory explains not only that the bread and wine become Christ's body and blood — but why this is so important for the believer. He notes that all human life is sacred. But the revealed fact that this life is not destroyed, merely changed, makes life all the more holy. The Divine Sacrament is the means we have been given by the Author of life to see to it that our life becomes complete. For the God of human life in creation and the God of divine life in Redemption is one. Through the body and blood of the Eucharistic mystery our life becomes potentially divine. At Mass the water and wine are mixed to remind us that divinity and humanity, God and man, became united in Christ so that they could be one also in us. It is here that we see the glory of the calling to Christian life which is to complete the process begun at birth. What God has begun in conception he would one day through His body and blood bring to full perfection in a life that knows no end.

Nor was there any confusion in Gregory's mind that the Eucharist, with all its divine life-conferring power, is the result of the priestly power to consecrate at the altar. He notes: "He unites Himself with their bodies so that mankind too, by its union with what is immortal, may share in incorruptibility. And this He confers on us by the power of the blessing, through which He changes the nature of the visible elements into that immortal body" (*Address on Religious Instruction,* Eucharist, No. 37).

The greatest problems in life came to Gregory after his selection as Bishop of Nyssa in 372. From that date until he died in 395 he had not a minute of peace. The Arian war of nerves and political intrigue still went on. Soon Gregory was on the defensive — deposed from his see and left in banishment. However, with the passage of time and the change of political fortune, the Arians were not able to keep down Gregory nor keep alive the charges that had first been leveled against him. He returned to his see and continued until his death to preach God's Word.

Gregory Nazianzen, companion and lifetime friend of Basil and Gregory of Nyssa, was born in 329. His training included the great tradition of his day — rhetoric, philosophy and logic. He had been brought up in the family that had worked diligently at Nazianzus to assist the aged bishop with his duties there.

In 361, an event took place that was to change forever the life of Gregory and his peaceful scholarly existence. He was ordained. Apparently he submitted to great pressure in accepting Holy Orders, for he fled immediately thereafter to compose himself and prepare himself properly for his new sacred responsibilities. It was in apologizing for this flight that he wrote what amounts to a treatise on the priesthood which offers some very beautiful material on the nature and function of the priest.

His vision of the priesthood was one that included the overall view first of the Church and then of the sacraments which differentiate people within the Church.

All the faithful and the priests with the bishop share one faith and one mission. But the participation in the mission is according to degrees of sacramental life and calling. The calling of the Church is to participate in the mission of Christ. The sacrament of baptism admits one to the Church and impresses the believer with the need to actively carry on Christ's work. Baptism joins one to Christ and makes one the living sharer in His divine life and mission. But within the Church there is another sacrament that is concerned with the participation in Christ's mission. The Sacrament of Orders makes one a sharer in Christ's mission in a special and unique way.

By configuring the priest to Christ, the Sacrament of Orders makes of the priest an authentic, authoritative and special representative of Christ within the community of believers who themselves are already joined to Christ. As baptism distinguishes the priest from the rest of men by admitting him to the life of Christ, so Holy Orders distinguishes the priest from the rest of the faithful by joining him to Christ in a more full manner. Accordingly, we can say that the mission of Christ is not divided among His followers but that all within His Church participate in it. Some, however, are called to participate more fully. The principle of this differentiation is the Sacrament of Orders just as the initial principle of differentiation of the Church from the world is the sacramental life of baptism.

In whatever nominal terms the function and its minister were recognized, the sacred action of presenting Christ was seen as the work of selected men. The whole incarnational context of the Church demanded that men be the sharers in the priesthood of Christ as He had been in man's state and condition. Therefore, the Church, though always the principal instrument of Christ's plan of salvation, required specific men to receive and carry on the uniquely fuller powers that Christ wished to leave to His Church.

Within the Church that is differentiated into a hierarchical structure, the fullness of the Sacrament of Orders is found in the bishop. He is the source and sign of the unity of the Church in faith and charity. He is the principal person whose mission it is to teach and direct the faithful in matters spiritual. Priests share the mission of the bishop because they participate in sacred Orders and, therefore, in the mission and calling of the bishop. The bishops are to the Church today what the Apostles were to the early Church. The same relationship has been passed on in an unbroken line from the Apostles' day to our own and is an essential part of the structure of the Church. Because the bishop cannot reach all those committed to his care, he shares his priestly order with others, thus constituting a subordinate level of orders.

The priest shares in a permanent way the Orders he receives in ordination. The call to priestly duty and service is not a temporary one. It is rooted in the identification of the priest with Christ. As Christ's Incarnation required a total giving of self, so the priest's participation in the extension of Christ's mission requires a complete and permanent self-giving.

Because the priest is identified with Christ and His mission, he receives in ordination a permanent designation and differentiation within the Church. Both the priesthood and the witness to the coming perfection of the Kingdom of God share a permanence that emanates from Christ's one and final revelation and His irrevocable union with His Church.

The life of Gregory was again deeply changed by another ordination. In 380, the Emperor Theodosius converted and was baptized. To calm things and promote the true faith, the emperor decided to clean out Constantinople. The people were told to accept only the faith approved by the Pope. The Arian bishop was given the option of conversion or early retirement. He seemed to have chosen the latter. Next, Theodosius chose Gregory for the post of bishop. The Cathedral of Constantinople — the cavernous Church of Holy Wisdom, dedicated to the Holy Spirit — was full of cheering people as Gregory accepted his new duties. And with zest he entered into the work as First Teacher of the Faith in the new imperial capital. But the termites were still busy.

Every possible argument was used against him. Slanders, lies, falsehoods of all sorts were created out of nothing and launched against him. The people were bewildered by this constant barrage of self-righteous half-truths against Gregory. Finally, the city was convulsed again in riot after an attempt was made on the bishop's life. Gregory, to save the city from further tumult and bloodshed, resigned. In the quiet of his retreat he wrote, preached and prepared for death, which came in 390. His remains were first taken from Nazianzus to Constantinople. They finally ended up in Rome, in St. Peter's Basilica.

Gregory was faced with several occasions when he had to summon up all his training in the classics, his considerable rhetorical ability and his undaunted faith. These occasions included the deaths of his brother Caesarius, his sister Gorgonia, his father and his dear friend Basil, whose deaths Gregory said left him "half dead" and have given the Church its most treasured funeral orations.

Gregory adapted the pagan funeral oration and made it a Christian teaching instrument. And he did it with such class that the four surviving orations are described as "masterpieces of Christian Greek funeral" oratory art.

The full import of the orations is that Christ is

risen. Therefore, we too will rise. Using the writings of St. Paul, Gregory paints a convincing picture of the Christian faith in the life to come — a personal life of the individual believer. Gregory relies heavily on the Letter of Paul to those of the faith at Corinth. He makes much of the references in Corinthians which speak of the Lord's death, burial and Resurrection.

The mention of the burial also implies, especially for anyone living at the time of this Epistle (c. 55-58), that the burial place is empty. In today's terminology this means that there was a control for the story, the Gospel, that Christ was risen. Not only does Paul call to witness the empty tomb, but he notes that a whole list of disciples saw the living Lord after the Resurrection.

"First and foremost, I handed on to you the facts which had been imparted to me: that Christ died for our sins, in accordance with the Scriptures; that He was buried; that He was raised to life on the third day, according to the Scriptures; and that he appeared to Cephas, and afterwards to the Twelve" (1 Corinthians 15:3-5).

But it seems that Paul's explanation to the Corinthians was not concerned with this point. They too accepted on faith and in faith that Christ, the Lord, was risen. They seemed more concerned with the ramifications of the Resurrection for others. The Corinthians, as Greeks, betrayed in this discussion their training and outlook which found a physical resurrection an absurdity. For them, Christ's Resurrection was one thing but the application of it across the board for others presented a position that jarred with their outlook. They were Greeks. Many of them were well acquainted with the writings of the great Greek philosophical tradition. And within that tradition the resurrection of the body had no place. If the Greeks, including those of Corinth, held any belief in an afterlife, they would think of it in terms of the immortality of the soul apart from the body. To them the body was the prison or cage of the soul that was destroyed in death. Death was a liberation of the soul but the extinction of the body.

Paul goes on in his Letter to explain that the Resurrection of Christ was a pledge to all believers that they, too, would rise. But the keystone of his whole argument is that first Christ is risen. "If there be no resurrection, then Christ was not raised" (1 Corinthians 15:24). Surely Paul, who had just finished relating the narrative of the death, burial and Resurrection of Christ, is not speaking of His Resurrection "in spirit" only. To the Corinthians he is preaching a bodily resurrection. It is precisely this bodily resurrection that they doubt. So Paul links every resurrection in glory to Christ's Resurrection in the flesh. "If Christ was not raised, then our Gospel is null and void and so is your faith" (1 Corinthians 15:17).

Not only does Paul stake the worth of his whole mission on the physical Resurrection of Christ but the validity of the entire Christian dispensation. The new order preaches not only Jesus resurrected from the land of the dead as the Christ — flesh and spirit, who walked the land of the living — but it preaches our resurrection from the dead because of Christ's. "We turn out to be lying witnesses for God because we bore witness that He raised Christ to life, whereas, if the dead are not raised, He did not raise Him" (1 Corinthians 15:15). The whole basis for belief in the resurrection of the dead is the Resurrection of Christ. That Resurrection is confirmed by the knowledge that Christ appeared to His disciples with a risen body after death. Without this fact, Christian faith is sterile and the Christian way of life a needless bother.

Gregory's funeral orations applied Christ's message, Christ's victory, St. Paul's message and the Church's teaching in a forceful, personal way. Like his life and faith, his work rings with deep-down intimate conviction.

Hilary of Poitiers

FATHER IN FRANCE

> He is the one through whom are things, and from whom are all things. . . . He is the Spirit of God, the Gift given to the faithful.
>
> —St. Hilary
> 'On the Trinity' (Book 2, No. 29)

Aquitaine stretches from the hills west of the Rhone River across the plains and open spaces of Southern France until it reaches the Atlantic Ocean. From the earliest days of Rome's gradually growing Empire, Aquitaine had enjoyed much notoriety. Its fields were verdant, its wines superb, and the weather for the most part mild. It is not therefore all that surprising to learn that it was selected by many a retiring legionnaire as the place where he would set up a home with his military service behind him.

The idea of pensioning off warriors to a place in the country was an old one with Rome. Julius Caesar made great use of it long before the legions were as numerous as they came to be. In his time, the pen-

sioners received land in the south of Italy. So many of
his old troopers were there that by the time of his
death, his heir, Octavius — later Caesar Augustus —
was able to produce almost overnight an army as he
passed through this land of small farmers.

Now, centuries later, Southern France was a
land of retired soldiers. Little farms dotted the coun-
tryside. The face of the Empire had changed radically
since the days of the Julian family. Now the full glory
of the royal light shone on the family of Constantine.
And by the year St. Hilary was born, the decision of
Constantine to become a Christian was already well
noised about.

What we know about Hilary is taken in the main
from references to him in St. Jerome and St. Augustine. As for his conversion to the faith, we learn of it
in the opening part of his treatise on the Trinity. Here
he tells us of how he was brought up in idolatry and
how step by step he came to understand the Christian
message and finally accepted it. Hilary's conversion
was followed by a life of deep dedication to the faith
and the Church. Some time around the year 350,
which would have been his thirty-sixth year, he was
chosen Bishop of Poitiers. He accepted this post with
some reluctance. His natural talents were for poetry
and writing. He was not particularly drawn to the
world of polemics. In fact, in the first few years of his
episcopate he devoted his energy to preaching, teaching, writing and producing the still extant *Commentary on the Gospel of St. Matthew.* But Hilary's peace
was short-lived. Unlike the Eastern part of the Empire, the West had not been so involved in Arian
heresy. The fight was mainly an Eastern one, with all
the political overtones so associated with the Byzan-

100

tine Court. Now the plague reached Italy and then Gaul and finally the reaches of Aquitaine.

Constantius, the heir in the line of Constantine, was a firm promoter of the new religion — Arianism. In spite of his position, he did not hesitate to remove bishops, banish them and call synods, councils and other clerical meetings to spread his convictions. To this end the emperor called for a meeting of bishops in Milan in 355. Milan had by this time taken the political lead in Western Europe that Rome once held. At his gathering, Constantius required the bishops to attack St. Athanasius and to sign a condemnation of him. A few refused. These were banished.

At this news, Hilary wrote to the emperor protesting this abuse of imperial power and pointing out the errors in the Arian heresy. Again the imperial thunderbolt flew. Constantius ordered his second-in-command, Julian, to banish Hilary. And so in 356, Hilary followed the footpath of so many bishops and priests of that period. In leaving his exiled home, the Bishop of Poitiers wrote again to Emperor Constantius and said, "I am a bishop, and notwithstanding exile I am in communion with all of the bishops of all of the churches of Gaul. Since you will not be able to find me guilty of any fault, even using the false report of those impious men that have denounced me, you send into exile an innocent person. I therefore must write to you because of the testimony of my own conscience. If it can be proved that I have done anything unworthy of the holiness of a bishop or even of the honesty of a layman, then I shall consider it my immediate duty to cease the exercise of my episcopal functions and take my place as a simple lay person in the midst of penitence" (Letter to Constantius, II, 2).

His exile was to last about three years, and during this time Hilary applied himself to his studies. The result is his now famous treatise, *On the Trinity*. To this work we shall return.

As seen in his Letter to Constantius, Hilary laid great emphasis on the communion of bishops. In a way, it was his version of collegiality. To the bishops of Gaul (now France, part of Switzerland and Germany) he wrote that their unity depended on their adherence to the faith, and that they remained in union only so long as they preached together the one same faith that they had received. "My most dear brothers, I have passed the limits within which any reckoning of my own ignorance could be contained, and for the love which I hold for all of you, I have been willing to forget my own sufferings. As a soldier of the Church, it is my duty, however, to call your attention by means of my letters to the voice of a bishop, that voice which is an echo of that of the holy Church and of the teaching of the Apostles. Now it is up to you acting in unity and with prudence to preserve in your own pure consciences the faith which up till now has been maintained intact" *(De Synodis)*.

Eventually, Hilary was summoned to attend the emperor's latest council or meeting of bishops. As distinct from an ecumenical Council which becomes one only as it is ratified by the Holy Father, the councils called by the emperors in the earlier centuries of the Church were usually regional meetings something like a meeting of a national conference of bishops today. This one was to be held in Seleucia. Its purpose was to neutralize the work of Nicaea. Unfortunately for those who organized this meeting, the exile had not destroyed Hilary's spirit. The same fires still burned that had produced the letter to Constantius. The meeting broke up with no great results except that Hilary had several excellent opportunities to let off steam. He returned eventually to Gaul where he outlived Constantius and died some time around 368. Pius XI in 1851 proclaimed him a Doctor of the Church.

Hilary lived at a time of great theological debate. The confusion was general among the hierarchy. There were meetings, synods, gatherings and councils of bishops held with a head-reeling speed and regularity. The imperial transport system — by which the bishops traveled free — complained that the system was cluttered with bishops traveling to and from meetings at which they disputed the same points disputed at their last meeting.

Much of the problem had its origin with Arius. Then came Nicaea with the Church's answer. However, not all were happy with the reply of Nicaea. It appeared to some that it led the Church down an unpopular street, particularly in the light of the imperial convictions concerning Christ.

Out of all this came many a work on the nature of Christ — His relationship to the Father and the place of the Holy Spirit in all of this. Hilary's treatise on the Holy Trinity is one of the first, however, to provide a really systematic treatment of the question.

The place of the Son as equal and eternal with the Father had been clearly stated by Nicaea. It spoke of the Son as of the same substance, *homo-ousion,* of the Father. Hilary explained at great length the meaning of what the Church teaches about the Sonship of Christ; he discusses the disputed point and tries to give it a coherent explanation. But perhaps one of his greatest contributions remains in the context of his treatise *On the Trinity*, his discussion on the Holy Spirit. To avoid what caused so much trouble in earlier works on the nature of Jesus and His relation to the Eternal Father, Hilary decided to keep his treatise on the Spirit well grounded in Sacred Scripture. He begins his short study with St. John's Gospel, Chapters 14, 15 and 16.

To those who keep the faith, to those who hold firm to Christ, will be sent the "Paraclete." He will have, as St. John sees it in Chapter 14, two major works to perform. He will lead men to the faith, and be their teacher; He will be to them the presence of Christ and giver of that faith. The Spirit is the teacher of the faith. In this capacity He gives the faith; then He explains, in the sense that He makes real in the life of the believer, the same faith. But He is also the very thing to which the faith is directed — the presence of God. He is the fuller life to which the faith leads. Once one has the faith, one shares the new life. To believe is then not only to feel the effects of the Paraclete as "teacher" but to "know" Him as the presence of God.

We find the Spirit given two names — Paraclete and Spirit of Truth. "If you love me and keep my commandments, then at my request the Father will give you another Paraclete to be with you forever. He is the Spirit of Truth. . . ." Here the Spirit is seen as the gift of the Father through Jesus to those who love Jesus and follow His commandments. We can see the nature of the work of the Paraclete Spirit by seeing in Him the work that Jesus carried on. That, precisely, was the work of intercessor and teacher. The difference, however, is that Jesus carried on an earthly work. The Paraclete Spirit will differ from Jesus in that the Spirit is not corporeally visible and His presence will only be by indwelling in the disciples.

As Jesus taught His disciples and through His commandments brought them to a new way of life, so will the Paraclete, once Jesus is "gone" from this world, teach through His indwelling and bring men to the fullness of life. The Spirit, the Paraclete, is meant to be the permanent presence of Jesus.

Somehow Jesus was to remain with His followers and carry on the same work that He was sent originally to do. His death did not stop Him. The Resurrection was His victory over death's power to prevent His work of witnessing the Father. But His physical presence after the Resurrection was to be short-lived. If He were to be with men and work with them, some other presence would have to be realized. Here was the place and work of the Spirit Paraclete. Jesus indicates He is to leave this world. But He will not leave His disciples forever. Moreover, He indicates that He will return to them. "I am coming back to you."

Here we find one of the functions of the Spirit. He is to take His place in the believer. He is to be the permanent presence of Christ. But He is also to be the teacher of the believer who makes the "seeing" of Christ possible. "You will see me."

What Christ is promising and giving to His disciples is the presence of God. The Spirit is to be both the teacher or "giver" of peace and Christian salvation as well. For by His presence the Spirit creates in the believer the "salvation," the "victory," the "righteousness" that is the presence of God. Harmony with God in the acts of the believer will follow from this initial bestowal of peace.

The entrance into the new life of Christ is the acceptance of the presence of the Spirit. In this sense the references to continued union with Christ make sense. By accepting faith one is united to Christ in a new life. But it is the Spirit, "Love," that constitutes that new life. One remains on in that love through the indwelling of the Spirit.

In terms of the disciple, the Spirit of Truth is the source of the believer's witness. Here we touch on one of the continuing actions of the Spirit that should be visible in the life of each believer. Witness is a fruit of the presence of the Spirit. And as such it should be visible to "the world." "The world will attempt to destroy the witness." "They are going to put you out of the Synagogue. In fact, the hour is coming when the man who puts you to death will think he is serving God." But the witness is not to abandon his task on account of the danger to himself. "I have said this to you to prevent your faith from being shaken."

Under the heading "The Paraclete," we see the Spirit as the great bearer of the faith. He it is who brings to the would-be believer the faith, while at the same time He takes up a place in the believer as the presence of God, the fruit of the faith. In theological terms the Spirit is the inspiration to faith, the source of grace and the indwelling of the Divine Presence. For St. John He is the Paraclete whom "the Father will give you to be with you forever."

In terms of the history of man's redemption the Spirit is the abiding presence of Christ in the Church. The work that Jesus came to do is now continued in the institution He established and identified with Himself. To make viable the Church, Jesus poured out the Spirit on her that she might be both home of

106

the Spirit and mother of the faithful. The believer finds Jesus in and through the Spirit. It is the permanent presence of the Spirit that constitutes the new life of the believer. And this new life is found only within the Church that Jesus founded.

As the "Spirit of Truth" we see the Spirit in St. John in His terrifying role as judge. Once men have been given the life there is no backtracking. Men either "live in the light" or they do not. The judgment against those who do not is rendered by the mere presence of the Spirit. There is no ignoring the mighty redemptive act of God in Jesus. It does not go away just because it is not accepted. To those who do accept Jesus, "life in the light" is given. For those who do not, the judgment of the Spirit awaits them. But His presence in the world, as Jesus' abiding through the Resurrection, is already acting as a judgment against those who will not accept Him.

Of course, Hilary had not said everything there is to say about the Holy Spirit, His distinctness, His consubstantiality with the Father and the Son and His indwelling within the believer. However, what he did write along with the work of St. Augustine did have a great influence. The "creed" of the Eleventh Council of Toledo (A.D. 675) is based on the writings of both Augustine and Hilary.

Hilary was conscious of his obligation to teach the faith. He wrote: "In addition to the obligation of my vocation and office as a bishop of the Church, I must indeed devote myself to the ministry of preaching the Gospel. I was the more inclined to assume the burden of writing, the more threatening was the danger of so many who were being held by the false belief." In fulfilling his duties, Hilary suffered exiles, the displeasure of the ruling civil administration, the loss of friends in the episcopate and a general rough time at the hands of his adversaries. But out of all of this he left for the Church in Gaul and the Church universal an example of service and precision teaching.

Ambrose

CHURCH DIPLOMAT

> That would be the most wretched thing of all,
> one's conscience bound and one's lips closed.

> — St. Ambrose
> 'Letter to the Emperor
> Theodosius' (No. 51)

Not many men were called to take on the awesome job of bishop while still laymen. Fewer still faced the work with the fearful respect and reverence as Ambrose. Yet so fell his lot.

Ambrose was the son of a Roman citizen in the service of the Empire. His father was prefect of Gaul. Ambrose followed in his father's footsteps, and he was, after his education in Rome, named governor of Liguria and Emilia — central Italy. He lived in Milan, which was the real, vital center of Italy. Ambrose was not yet out of his thirties when he took on this post, but he seemed to have a disposition and a sensibility that resisted rash solutions and violent changes. In his new office, the young Ambrose worked with an impartiality and fairness not easily found in some public officials. He soon came to be noted for his honesty. However, in God's providence, his integrity was soon to be put to more important work than that of administering the laws of a fading Empire.

It happened in 374 that the Bishop of Milan died. Auxentius had been an Arian and for nearly twenty years had been Bishop of Milan. That city, like so many throughout the Empire, was torn between the Catholic and the Arian teachings. The one great legacy of this heresy, as others in its wake, was its ability to divide Christians from Christians and make of God's holy Church a cheap debating room where any type of politically, financially or personally advantageous offer took preference to the truth. Milan was now divided by these Christian parties, each desiring to elect the new bishop. The election date was set and a place was chosen. It was to be held in a large church in the central part of the town. Both sides escalated arguments. Someone called the police. Ambrose arrived. To calm the people and to remind them of their Christian duties, he gave a short talk. The theme was peace. He prayed for understanding. The outcome was totally unexpected. Someone in the crowd shouted, "Ambrose for bishop!"

The idea caught on, and soon Ambrose found himself confronted with his own selection as bishop; both parties, Arians and Catholics, proclaimed him. Needless to say, the most surprised was Ambrose. First of all, he was by some accounts not yet baptized, although he practiced the faith. He rejected the acclamation and returned to his home. But in consequence of the remarkable demonstration in the

Church, the bishops of the province ratified the election. Ambrose wrote immediately to the emperor that this was foolishness. He noted that Church law should not be overcome by emotionalism.

Valentinian, however, had another idea. Cynically, he wrote that he was pleased that the provincial governors he appointed were worthy of being bishops. Thus it came about that Ambrose was consecrated on December 7, 374, at the age of thirty-five. Thus it also happened that like Becket and Henry II, once friends, so Ambrose and his emperor, now friends, would soon come to blows over God's Church and her rights.

What we know of Ambrose's life as a bishop we learn at firsthand from the deacon Paolino, who was his devoted secretary and who went with him on his various travels. Thanks to this young cleric, we also have some insight into the character of Ambrose. He was by nature a disciplined man, a measured man, and a reasonable man. He was almost a natural for the eventual role of diplomat within the Church.

We recall that Ambrose protested his appointment as bishop. He wrote the emperor that he who was not born in the Church nor nourished by her should hardly be expected to become her priest. But the emperor obliged him in any case to accept the post. Cola writes that all Ambrose's training in the world of politics and diplomacy stood him well in his new post as bishop. Perhaps the emperor really understood this. For what had been his natural ability and political acumen could now be elements of his new zeal placed at the disposition of the Gospels. One of the first confrontations which followed on his consecration was with the very man who had imposed it on him. Some of the civil magistrates in Milan were acting with a callous disregard for truth and justice. Ambrose wrote to the emperor. Valentinian replied rather evasively that he was aware of the freedom of speech that Ambrose allowed himself and hoped that the new bishop would apply those remedies to the sins around him prescribed by God's law. The sometimes warm, sometimes cold, sometimes even heated relationship between the emperor and the bishop came to an end in 375, when Valentinian received a mortal wound in battle. He died on November 17 that year.

Now the Empire had a plethora of emperors and co-emperors. Valens, the brother of the dead emperor, was co-emporer in the East. Gratian, the son of the dead emperor, was co-emperor in the West, and his half-brother Valentinian II also claimed to be co-emperor. While these scurried about gathering forces to support them in some sort of eventual showdown, the state of the Empire worsened. The Goths were invading Roman territories, and some semblance of unity was badly needed. The divided parties turned to Ambrose. And our man took on the mantle of diplomat at court. His first work of reconciliation was followed by a line of successful diplomatic missions which culminated in his intervention with Valentinian II. In order to spare the life of a usurper and keep the forces of the Empire at peace, Ambrose responded to his new diplomatic calling with great zest.

Apparently he saw in his diplomatic work a real priestly function. For him, either the Empire would initiate a reform — a real Christian reform — in which all men would benefit, or the Empire would continue its downhill slide. Writing to Gratian, the co-emperor, he says that where faith in God has been violated, so faith in the Empire is lessened. His object was to make of the State a worthy vehicle for the faith, which in turn would unify all men in peace. To this same end — the peace and freedom of men — he put to use his personal goods. In the fighting with the Goths, large numbers of Italians, especially from around Milan, were taken prisoner. Ambrose entered into negotiations immediately for their release. The reply was money: Give us money and lots of it, and we will give you back the prisoners.

To meet the bill, Ambrose took the unprecedented step of melting down the sacred vessels in the churches of Milan and converting them into transportable ingots of silver and gold. In this manner he brought back from slavery large numbers of Italians. He also brought on his own head the criticisms of those who claimed that God's treasures should not be squandered to meet momentary demands. His reply is extant. Ambrose wrote among other things contained in his reply to the Arian detractors: "It is better to conserve a soul for God than gold for a temple. The One who sent the Apostles out without gold has also founded His Church without gold, and if now this same holy Church possesses gold, it is not to conserve it that it has it but to use it for those who are in difficulty" (*De Officiis,* II, 28).

Ambrose did not limit his diplomatic offensive on behalf of the Church solely to those in prison or on the slave block. He pleaded for understanding on all levels of the imperial court and for those in it of other religious attitudes. When news reached him of a pagan councillor at court who was sentenced to death for *lèse majesté* (offending the emperor), Ambrose pleaded his cause. When the old Dowager Empress Justina — an Arian and a long-time enemy of Ambrose's, and a person, who in the words of one writer, "suffered almost hysterically from the mere fact of Ambrose's existence" — when she needed help to keep her son's head in place, it was Ambrose who traveled to Trier in Germany to meet with the emperor and smooth over problems. And thus another diplomatic mission was satisfactorily completed. These missions cost Ambrose much in strength and energy but won him and the Church some peace. In the meantime, the faith made headway. Gratian at Ambrose's request removed from the Senate House the pagan altar of victory and gave up once and for all the ancient Roman title now reserved solely to the Pope: *Pontifex Maximus* (Supreme Pontiff).

However, one of the greatest ironies of providence in the life of Ambrose began with the good news in 379 that Flavius Theodosius had been appointed by Gratian co-emperor in the East. Theodosius was a Catholic and a deeply convinced one. In the course of time he settled the problem of the Goths in the Balkans. Eventually Gratian was slain and Theodosius avenged his death by defeating the last contender to the throne. Finally Theodosius ruled, sole and supreme emperor of all the domain of Rome. In the course of his many campaigns, Theodosius had demonstrated a military ability and a terrific temper, and so his soldiers were not at all abashed when in a campaign in Greece, the emperor had punished a treacherous and traitorous village when he massacred the entire population of 7,000. Theodosius was, however, greatly surprised to find that his friend Ambrose had declared him, Theodosius, emperor, guilty of public sin and in need of public penitence. No, Ambrose explained, His Majesty could not enter the church nor receive the sacraments nor attend services until suitable penance had been done.

Perhaps no single act so points up Ambrose's unflinching dedication to the truth. Little would have stopped the king from cutting Ambrose down where he stood. Centuries later, Henry II would do precisely that to Becket. Nor could Ambrose count on much gain in his stand. But the matter stood, and so did Ambrose. Theodosius did penance and peace was restored. In his later funeral oration over Theodosius, Ambrose recalled the whole event and the emperor's faith and penance. "He stripped himself of every sign of royalty and bewailed his sin openly in church. He, an emperor, was not ashamed to do public penance which lesser individuals avoid, and to the end of his life he never ceased to repent his mistake" (*On Theodosius,* 34).

No doubt the easy access to the corridors of power and his free passage through the offices of public administration must have turned Ambrose to consider the mixing of his duties — priest and bishop — with those of public official and politician. In fact, prior to his ordination he had been just that, a politician and a good one. But in his new office, Ambrose set a standard that insisted on the separation of the two posts for the good of God's Church and the spread of the Gospels.

Ambrose knew that the priest's witness will always touch the political, social, cultural and economic orders. This is true because his message must touch men where they are. But the question is, "How does he make his witness felt?" Few would say that the priest is to exercise no influence in the world of politics. After all, he is part of the larger community and a spokesman for some of its most cherished principles. In his preaching and in other situations, he necessarily will make clear the moral imperatives that are part of the Gospel message. This means that at times the priest may find himself holding some positions that are also reflected in the public statements of certain politicians or in the platform of a given political party. Such coincidence cannot be avoided. In fact, one would hope that moral judgments expressing Christian values would often be found in the programs and statements of partisan politicians. But when they are not there, the question remains, "How do we see to it that politics and Christian imperatives are mingled?"

Ambrose understood that the priest is to teach, plead, influence and exhort his fellow Christians. On the level of his healing ministry he is to be a witness to the ultimate unity of all men and the law of love that must eventually embrace all peoples. To do this may require opposition to some government statements or programs. But such opposition is best rendered "how?" By the imposition of laws drawn up by priests? By the negotiation of priest-politicians with party bosses? Or should it rather be the influence of conviction? Should it rather be the Christian faith's power to move men — even in public life — to follow Christ's way?

To those not consecrated to minister to the people in God's name is given the task of politically working out a just society. The priest is seen as a man of God for all the people. He cannot devote his energies to partisan political activities and still carry out his original and consecrated commitment. It is a question of priorities. The priest has made a promise. He is obliged by his own decision and choice to give himself to all the believing community as God's man among men. Such a self-giving is a necessary step in passing on to the next generation the Good News of Christ.

For the layman, consecrated in baptism, a different set of priorities pertain. His family, his job should be the practical means through which he builds God's Kingdom. As an engineer, a soldier, a farmer or a worker he can concentrate on one aspect of the civil order. As a politician he can give himself to a specifically limited political philosophy. In doing so he equally does God's will and establishes here and now a glimpse of the glory of God's Kingdom.

No one, least of all the Church, says that because of his commitment or set of priorities the priest has lost his right to political activity. A monk who fasts certainly has not lost his natural right to food. A consecrated virgin is not devoid of the human right to marry. But both are examples of the application in the practical order of a spiritual commitment. They live a set of priorities that make intelligible the renunciation of certain natural appetites. So, too, the priest. He is not denied his civil rights. But the desire to enter active politics is subordinated to a higher task — a more universal work. As a consecrated witness to the Gospel the priest cannot afford to get bogged down in a partisan political fight. The community needs more his power to unite and his ability to heal than it does his ability in ward politics.

The priest is responsible to the Gospels. He is a spokesman for the Church. As a public figure in the

Church he is expected to teach what the Church teaches. This is all the more so even if his congregation may not appreciate at any given moment a specific teaching. The Gospel message cannot be filtered through voter appeal. The practical force of this argument is clear when any priest seeking a political office might find it necessary to oppose the concretely expressed teaching of the Church. In this case even the candidate admits that the Church's teaching must give way to the other preference of the voting majority in his party. Prophetic witness is thus muffled in political expediency; priestly dedication yields to the partisan.

Ambrose was well aware of the fact that his witness or the strength of it was precisely because he walked wide of political intrigues. Even when offered political power in Milan at the height of one of the many insurrections, he was careful to explain to the excited crowds that his work as a bishop was quite different from what his work as a civil governor had been and that they could never be made to mix.

On January 16, 395, Theodosius died in the city of Ambrose: Milan. The funeral oration of Ambrose, though in plan a praise of the faith and virtue of the emperor, also contained undertones of misgiving. This anxiety is seen in the repeated appeals to the army to keep the peace, to permit a peaceful transition of power and order. But the shadows of gathering dark clouds were already visible. Two years later, Ambrose died — April 4, 397. And slowly the doors of history closed shut on an era — the era of empire and the age of Ambrose.

Augustine

FATHER OF GRACE

Honor, love and praise the holy Church, your mother, the heavenly Jerusalem, the holy City of God. It is she who, in this faith which you have received, bears fruit and spreads throughout the world. She is the Church of the living God, the pillar and mainstay of truth.

> —*St. Augustine*
> *'For Recent Converts' (Sermon 214, No. 11)*

In 354 in the small town of Tagaste in northern Africa near Hippo was born St. Augustine. And all around him, a world and a way of life nearly 500 years old was crumbling. Even at this early date, but certainly by his death in 430, it was increasingly apparent that the Empire of Rome was dying. The line of emperors descending from Constantine the Great would peter out in blood-splashed civil wars which saw Roman legions fighting each other while all the time the enemies of Rome crept closer. Before he was to die at Hippo in a city besieged by the Vandals, Augustine would see the leadership of the Roman Empire pass from the Constantinian line to several emperors supported by factions of the army, to Theodosius, who checked the decay momentarily, to a division of the Empire into East and West.

In the same period of roughly eighty years, he would see Roman armies surrendering to the Persians (366 A.D.), routed by the Goths on the Danube (378) and withdrawn from Britain (407). All along the long, thin line of legionnaires that kept mighty Rome from the forces that lurked outside her pale, inroads were being made. The Goths ravaged the once prime provinces of the Balkans. Vienna, the proud Roman outpost, where Marcus Aurelius died, was now in the hands of the Goths. The Franks murdered the Roman governor at Vienna and set up their own. The Vandals and numerous other groups swarmed across Rome's once impregnable borders. Finally, on August 14, 410, Alaric and the Huns sacked Rome. Rome, which until the reign of Aurelius had not even thought of building walls to protect itself; Rome, whose proconsuls' words had been law throughout the Mediterranean world for 300 years; Rome, whose parasitic population had swollen to over a million in the days of bread and circuses — Rome had fallen.

Into this world was born the son of Monica, a Christian, and Patricius, a pagan. In these changing currents Augustine grew, was educated, spent his youth, was converted, and wrote what was to be Africa's greatest legacy to the Church.

The life of Augustine or at least his early years, which had a certain libertine cast, is well-known to readers of his *Confessions*. He left Hippo, his birthplace, at the age of seventeen, where he took up the student occupations of study and carousing. Having mastered his subjects and fathered a child, Augustine took on the more serious work of teaching, which he did with great success. However, in 383 he left Northern Africa for Rome and eventually Milan. By this time Milan was the important city in Italy. Rome still stood on the Tiber, but fewer and fewer emperors even visited it. Milan offered civil and commercial opportunities. It also boasted of one of the greatest of bishops — Ambrose.

It was while at Milan that Augustine, under the influence of Ambrose and other Christian friends and the prayers of his mother, was converted. The story of this odyssey is contained in the volumes of his *Confessions*. This work we owe in no small part to the request made by another famous churchman in Italy. Paulinus of Nola is believed to have requested of Augustine the initial material that later grew into the now famous *Confessions*.

On the vigil of Easter in 387, St. Ambrose, Bishop of Milan, performed what might be called his most important work for the Church: he baptized Augustine. And the recent excavations under the massive Italian-Gothic Cathedral of Milan have unveiled not only the ancient baptistery of Ambrose but the foundations of his catechetical school in which so many were led to the faith.

Following his baptism, Augustine and Monica, along with several others of their party, including his son, who was now nearly fifteen, started back to Africa. At one stop along the way Monica died. Again archaeology offers us some witness. At Ostia, the ancient seaport of Rome, we find in the extensive excavations the home reputed to be the place of Monica's death. Augustine devoted an impressive part of his *Confessions* to the quiet, forceful, believing woman who was his mother.

Not long after his return to Africa, Augustine was consecrated bishop, then acted as auxiliary bishop to Valerius, whom he eventually succeeded. For thirty-five years then as Bishop of Hippo, Augustine taught the faith, defended the faith and gave to the Church a vision of the world of faith — *The City of God.* His pen seemed never dry. He wrote continual commentaries on the Bible, philosophical treatises, cultural tracts, articles on just about every conceivable subject, and reams of letters. Outstanding and for centuries normative were his works on the Trinity, grace and creation. His sermons fill volumes. Out of this explosion came *The City of God,* which Etienne Gilson calls "not only one of Augustine's masterpieces but among the classics of all literature."

To the crumbling political structures of the then known world, Augustine in his *City of God* was offering the vision of a world one in faith, one in vision, one in spiritual unity. The days of the politically unified Empire were gone. In fact, in less than fifty years after the death of Augustine, the reign of the last even nominal Roman emperor came to an end. Gilson reminds us that "the great Bishop of Hippo probably would never have written it *[The City of God]* except for the fall of Rome and the ensuing controversies to which that event gave rise." Augustine's vision, touched upon in his *Commentaries on the Sermon of the Mount,* was of a spiritual realm. He saw unity in peace, but peace only understood as the spiritual peace that is Christ's gift.

By involving men in a new ethical situation that contradicts their own experience, Christ set the stage for the working out of His peace. But He also watered the seeds of tension. In contrast to the pragmatic calculations and reasoned positions of the Greeks and Romans, Jesus spoke of a personal commitment in charity towards all men. So revolutionary and demanding is this commitment that it depends utterly on a perspective offered only by revelation. And so the Christian peace is part of, as well as the result of, revelation. But it is a revelation that must be acted on in terms of this world (Luke 12:49). We can affirm that there are different varieties of peace that are mentioned in the Gospels (John 14:27). But in practical terms when dealing with the question of peace among men and its attainment in this life we have to admit that the peace which Christ came to give the world is intimately tied in with the practical peace among men that He also demands (Matthew 5:23-24). This peace is found only in the world as seen through the perspective that Christ came to offer.

Matthew outlines, in the several chapters that make up the Sermon on the Mount, some of the essential attitudes that are the result of the new perspective. The Gospel insists on a vision of man as an eventual citizen of heaven. The balance it sets is between works of the social order and those directed to another world. The background is always human life seen as potentially divine and eternal. It proclaims peace in the same breath with which it blesses poverty and mourning. Believers are reminded of their duties to the poor, the afflicted, the downtrodden, but always in terms of the Kingdom of Heaven. The perspective is that of their vocation as sons of God. They are to build up this world because they are called to see God. Within this view both God and man have value in themselves.

The Sermon on the Mount requires that the believer see his fellowman's dignity. This dignity comes from God, resides in man and is held sacred because of man's ultimate goal, union with God. But such a perspective requires faith. Belief alone makes it possible for a man to hold out hope in the life to come. Faith provides the moral climate, in which, for the Christian, human dignity can assert itself and human freedom can grow.

Augustine saw the Church's role in the new spiritual order as essential. She was to be the new unifier, the new source of peace and spiritual order. It is the duty of the Church to nourish and feed the fragile peace that has been conceived by Christ and born in His Church. This is done in the context of a world only partly perfect — only on the way to its goal of perfection in Christ. The Church, God's only flock, like a standard lifted high for the nations to see, ministers the Gospel of peace as she makes her pilgrim way in hope towards her goal, the Fatherland above.

Christ gave men His peace. But He did not outline each detail of the road that leads to its full possession. In fact, He spoke of it as if it were not a peace with which we are familiar. Part of the problem for the Christian in attaining this gift is precisely that of defining exactly the peace that Christ offers. This is so since His peace seems to involve some ambiguity. It even seems to be contradictory to what might be called a pacifist or "nonviolence" position.

Tension is found in Christ's multiple position with regard to force and peace. He obviously did not equate it with coexistence or temporary armistice. The voices in the Gospel tell us that Jesus saw peace as many-sided. In Matthew (chapter 26, verse 52), Christ warns against the use of force. Yet He applies it Himself as He clears out the temple (John 2:14-17). At times His position even seems threatening.

"Do not suppose that I have come to bring peace to the earth: it is not peace I have come to bring, but a sword. For I have come to set a man against his father, a daughter against her mother, a daughter-in-law against her mother-in-law. A man's enemies will be his own household" (Matthew 10:34-36).

He told His followers to be peacemakers but reminded them that His peace is not of this world. In the Sermon on the Mount Jesus announced what He would ask of His followers. He stated the new level of ethical awareness He would demand from the members of His Kingdom. His peace was to be a challenge.

"You have heard that it was said of the people in the old days, 'Thou shalt not kill.' . . . I say to you that anyone who is angry with his brother must stand trial. . . . 'Thou shalt love your neighbor and hate your enemy' . . . but I say to you, love your enemies, and pray for those who persecute you" (Matthew 5:21-29).

But for Augustine, the City of God will never be fully realized as is the City of Man. Gilson again writes that from the point of view of Augustine himself, *The City of God* tells a tale which will end with the final triumph of the City of God — the ultimate end and true final cause of the divine work of creation. We are only starting to build, and the final edifice will be completed only in Heaven. Our world is one of tension between the City of God here and the heavenly Jerusalem yet to come.

For the Christian, peace involves a tension. The radical tension is founded, first of all, on the imperfect state of man. He is not yet at complete ease with God and therefore can and does reject divine guidance. Man can substitute his plans for those of God. This is all the more disastrous since at times he seems to succeed all the better without invoking supernatural explanation or assistance. With secular means he can establish real intervals of tranquillity. He might even eradicate momentarily the harshness of war without even a nod toward the Word of God. But this peace is a passing one. Jeremiah decried the fake prophets who yell, "peace, peace," when there is no peace. His position, again reflecting the later Christian ethic, was that only truth and justice can make peace.

The Christian position on peace is all the more delicate because of the ambiguities involved in the Christian view of life. As he awaits the second coming of Christ, the believer has all the advantages of knowing where he is going and the drawback of not yet having arrived. In this sense he is called "pilgrim," "wayfarer," traveler with "no lasting city." Christ once lived among us and has given to our activities a new direction and meaning. But the selfish side of human nature can thwart both God's plan and man's best efforts. It is in the large area between what is and what can be that tension develops. The true peace and well-being of each man will rest upon his relationship to God. Yet even with the redemption and the Church to carry on Christ's work, man's relationship with God is a fragile and a very incomplete one. All the seeds for perfection are there. But they still need a great deal of cultivating. St. Paul used the figure of the old man struggling with the new one to point out that man is not yet fully saved even though his redemption has been won. He can still opt for a choice that offends God's plan and man's dignity.

If Augustine hoped to see in this world some unified kingdom based on man's spiritual communion, perhaps he shared a dream with Dante, who followed him centuries later. Perhaps he even dreamed of a Christendom like Dante's world of one Pope with a spiritual order and one emperor for the temporal. But in any case, as he closed his eyes to this world in death, unity was but a dream. At the very doors of his city lay the siege machines, sappers' tools and attack weapons of the Vandals — just one of the many tribes that were rending to pieces the purple cloak of Imperial Rome. Soon Hippo, Carthage and finally all of Africa would be lost first to the civilized world and then to the faith. Only the vision created by Augustine endured to give men hope and light.

Paulinus of Nola

FATHER WITH FRIENDS

It is honorable to confess the works of the Lord. This is my reason for writing this letter. . . .

—*St. Paulinus of Nola*
'To Macarius' (Letter 49)

The world that made up the Roman Empire was largely settled around the Mediterranean Sea. It let out most of that part of Europe that was later to show its genius in Gothic cathedrals, Shakespeare, Wagner, Beethoven and the North American colonizers. But the Empire had a different face than the one we see when we look to the Mediterranean today. Now we find individual nations each following more or less its own course. Then there was but one nation, one state. The difference perhaps can best be seen in the little things. When, for example, Paulinus of Nola who died an old man in 431 was crisscrossing the world of his day he never needed to stop for custom control, passport check, national visa or change of currency. In his travels across Spain, France, Italy and elsewhere he was always a "citizen," a "local," never a "foreigner" or "stranger."

Paulinus was born in Bordeaux, Southern France. It seems that his family was rather well off because his father left him properties in France and Spain, as well as at Nola in Italy where Paulinus and his wife finally settled down. Everybody knew Paulinus. In his travels and in his work he made many a friend. And to keep alive those friendships he carried on a huge letter-writing campaign. He wrote to Ambrose, Augustine, Jerome and just about everybody who would have been in the "Who's Who" of the hour.

Fortunately for us, a good part of this correspondence has been preserved. From it not only can we piece together Paulinus' life but we can learn a great deal of the customs of the time, the theological preoccupations, spiritual concerns and general interests of a remarkable age that contained Augustine, Ambrose and Paulinus.

Ordination came to Paulinus late in life and by a rather curious route. His initial preference was for poetry and literature. He could, given his family's condition, afford to play the "gentleman of leisure." But he worked for a living following in the path of his father as a civil servant. His job, which seems to have been something like that of a comptroller, caused him to travel around a great deal and visit the Western Empire — Gaul, the Iberian Peninsula and Italy. While in Spain Paulinus married and eventually converted to the faith. This he took with great seriousness and began selling much of his property, goods and holdings to provide for the poor.

It was at this point that ordination came upon

our man. Perhaps it is best to read his own description of the whole event; writing to Sulpicius Severus, a long-time friend, Paulinus says: "As I wrote previously, I am now staying in the city of Barcelona. After my letter which you answered on the day on which the Lord designed to be born as man, I was ordained to the priesthood. The Lord witness that it happened through the sudden compulsion of the crowd, but I believe that I was forced into it at His command. I confess that I was unwilling. Not that I despised the rank (for I call the Lord to witness that I longed to begin my holy slavery with the name and office of sacristan), but since I was bound elsewhere and had my mind, as you know, firmly intent on another place, I trembled at this strange and unexpected decree of the divine will" (Letter 1, No. 10).

So noted had the charity and generosity of Paulinus become that the people by acclamation nominated him for sacred Orders. Thus he was ordained. The manner of his calling was not exactly under normal circumstances and later when Paulinus reached Rome he found his reception a bit cool. If the people of Spain thought that they had triumphed in the ordination of their favorite son they were not able to triumph too long. Paulinus was set and determined to return to Southern Italy. He had once served there as a civil district governor and had some property, including a farm at Nola not too far from Naples. It was here that he headed shortly after the ordination.

On his way to Nola Paulinus paid a visit to Rome. His letter, again to Severus, sounds almost like a modern-day pilgrim's account of so much to do and see in so little time: "I had only ten days to see the city, and saw nothing. The mornings I spent in prayer, the reason for my visit, at the sacred tombs of the Apostles and martyrs. Then, though I returned to my lodging, I was detained by countless meetings, some caused by friendship and some by duty. Our gatherings scarcely broke up and gave me relaxation in the evening" (Letter 17, No. 2).

On his arrival in Nola he sends off a letter in which he refers to the "cool" treatment his presence was afforded by the clergy of the Eternal City. He notes that they seem "to regard me as a stumbling block" (Letter 5, No. 13).

Whatever was his worth as seen by the clergy of Rome, at Nola there was never any question. For years Paulinus worked to revitalize the Christian community in a city that had many needs. More and more of his property was sold off to provide funds with which to help those in need. Soon a new church building went up to accommodate those coming to Mass. Finally Nola came to select a new bishop. In 409 the old bishop of the city died. And from that year until his death Paulinus carried on the work as the new "shepherd of a small flock." Apparently nothing about this set of circumstances upset the Roman clergy, for we hear no further of it in later correspondence.

In Paulinus' letters and those of his correspondents, we can gather up the elements that eventually help us to paint some sort of a picture of the Bishop of Nola. Certainly he was a man of great culture. His conversation was much appreciated, and it seems everyone wanted to carry on some communication with him. But another side of Paulinus comes out as we read his letters. He was a very humble man. He was a very spiritual man. And in his humility he was continually seeking advice that would further his growth in grace. Writing to Amandus, the priest who had been his catechist at Bordeaux, he states: "Your letters frequently give me the fresh resources that I need. For nourished up in the words of faith and of the good doctrine which you have attained in Sacred Scripture from boyhood, (I ask you to) fashion me in accordance with your rule of direction, feed me with the spiritual food which is the Word of God. . . . Do not because of my ordination be less careful in your care of my formation" (Letter 2, No. 3). At another time he writes to his same trusted confessor: "Christ is asleep within me. You must awake Him that He may arise to animate my soul" (Letter 9, No. 2).

On the more mundane side of things we see our man at Nola sending gifts to his friends and inquiring after their safe arrival. To Severus he writes: "I send you some Campanian bread as a blessing from our store . . . deign to receive this bread in the name of the Lord" (Letter 5, No. 21). One wonders at the speed of the postal service that bread could arrive still fresh. To another friend he writes of his gratitude for a work of Augustine sent him. His praise of the work is high: "I admire and revere it so much that I believe the words have been dictated by divine inspiration" (Letter 3, No. 2). But as any recipient, Paulinus intends to reply with a gift of his own. He informs his benefactor that "I have made arrangements for the great universal history of Eusebius (to be sent to you)." Another insight into the times is seen by the rest of this letter. Evidently the bookstores of Nola were not aways filled with the more substantial works. Paulinus notes that he had to write to Rome to get a copy of this "so worthy work."

But not all was light chatter in the writings of a man of such renown. His letters encourage some to write of his life and times. To Augustine he writes asking so many questions that eventually Augustine wrote his book on the *Care of the Dead*. Again to Augustine, prodding him to write against other enemies of the faith as he did against the Manichaeans, he writes: "If you have written any defenses of the Catholic faith against other enemies I beg you to provide me with arms of justice from your armory" (To Augustine, Letter 4, No. 2).

The underlying basis for the ease with which Paulinus carries on his correspondence and communications is again seen in his writings. He is convinced that all believers make up one body of Christ. He is persuaded that he is a brother of every believer and therefore can make requests of them, teach them, instruct them and open his heart in need to them. The explanation of this openness to his fellow Christians is found in St. Paul and his doctrine of the Mystical Body. Paulinus, writing to Augustine, makes this point with a clarity that one expects to find only in a document as well written as Pius XII's *Mystici Corporis*. "Nor is it surprising that we are together though apart, and acquainted though unknown to each other, for we are members of one body; we have one Head, we are steeped in one grace, we live on one Bread, we tread the same path, we dwell in the same house. In short, all that we are, in all the hope and faith in which we now stand as we strive for the future, is one in the spirit and body of the Lord; and if we break away from this unity, we are nothing" (Letter 6, No. 2).

The theology contained even in this one passage

of the Bishop of Nola is worthy of a study in depth. It speaks with simple conviction and open adherence to the belief in the Church as the Body of Christ. It makes no apology for the fact that outside this Body we "are nothing" and it lists the elements of the unity with Christ as our faith, the communion in the sacraments which give grace, the Eucharist and ecclesial union.

Later to Licentius, the same line of thought is continued with application to the political order: "There is one faith, one God, one Christ; and service to the Lord cannot be divided. For the gulf between the things and commands of Christ and those of Caesar is as great as that between Heaven and earth" (Letter 8, No. 3).

From Nola we might think that Paulinus was able to do little to advance his vision in faith of all men at one in Christ. But yet through his writings, his conversations, his charity and his example, he carried on in a great tradition that has long become part of the Church's appreciation of witness to the Word. From a diocese that today is lost in the environs of Naples, Salerno and Amalfi, he was able to make an impression on the Church and history that would justify a see the size of Chicago or Buenos Aires. By an untiring labor and ability to communicate — to make a point — Paulinus carried on an apostolate that perhaps is best summed up, at least in its purpose, in a line he wrote in a poem to Nicolas, the Bishop of Remesiana in Dacia, a famous missionary: "To Echo Christ with a Roman Heart." This same line now forms the motto on the coat of arms of the American Cardinal in Rome, John Cardinal Wright.

Leo and Gregory

THE 'GREAT' FATHERS

In order to pay the debt of our fallen state, inviolable nature was united to one capable of suffering (and that is the sort of reparation we needed); one and the same Mediator between God and men, the man Jesus Christ, could die in the one nature and not die in the other.

—*Pope St. Leo the Great*
'The Tome' (Letter 28)

History has granted to few men the judgment "great." Although nations, organizations and clubs freely grant distinctions, mankind through its living voice, history, is more sparing in its high praise. Of those proclaimed "great," we have such famous names as Alexander, Darius, Alfred, Charles (Charlemagne), Frederick and Catherine. The number has never been large. On two Popes, both within 150 years' time, this title rests — Leo the Great and Gregory the Great.

Leo was born at the turn of the fifth century. The

world of ancient Rome was dying. A new world was just beginning to dawn. And for his part in contributing to the new way of life, Leo came to be called "great." The sick form of the once proud Empire was divided in two. In the East, what remained of the Empire was centered in Constantinople. Emperors came and went, fought over doctrinal matters that pertained to the faith, warded off inter-palace plots, lost more ground to the barbarian advances, and displayed a general ineptitude. In the West, only the title remained. There was little more than a sham civil government.

The city of Rome was falling into chaos. Public services nearly stopped. Order was vanishing. Politicians, military men, civil figures receded into the background.

Against this backdrop worked Leo. Under several Popes he served as a deacon and was involved in the general financial affairs of the see of Rome. He seems to have demonstrated early in life his organizational talents and abilities in administration. His immediate predecessor, Sixtus III, died while Leo was exercising another of his skills — pacifier. Leo was in Gaul trying to get two rival generals to agree to stop fighting each other long enough to defend the frontier in what is now France. At the news of Sixtus' death, Leo returned to Rome, was chosen Pope and consecrated in September of 440. Thus began his reign of a little over twenty years. And thus began the seedwork for a new order which later Gregory the Great would nourish and water and help grow into Christian Western Europe.

Leo's great contribution in terms of the future of the Church's life and the survival of some culture and learning in Europe was twofold. He confirmed beyond doubt the place of Rome within the administrative, disciplinary, teaching, doctrinal complex that is the Church universal. He accepted the historical necessity of pulling together some civil government and leaving Europe some stability. He saw the Empire was dying. He could not help but see that. All around him there was the smell of decay. His job as he envisioned it was to provide a base for the future.

Probably the most remembered single work of Leo is the letter concerning the theological problems wracking the Eastern Empire. The letter read at the Council of Chalcedon is now called "The Tome of St. Leo." Technically, it is Letter No. 28. It confirmed, among other things, the right of the Holy Father to speak definitively on doctrinal matters even to the bishops, and it ended the confusion plaguing the Eastern Church.

Pope Leo's "tome" was a reply to Flavian, Bishop of Constantinople, who had written to the Pope, but whose letter was delayed in getting to Rome. Eventually, Leo's letter was read to the assembled bishops at the Council of Chalcedon. And their acceptance of his teaching was reflected in their acclamation, "Peter has spoken through Leo."

The "tome" presents many theological precisions, doctrinal positions and interesting points. In the last category we find the opening reminder or rebuke to those who in their studies and exegesis or in their lack of critical procedure had confused the faithful and tampered with the faith. Leo notes: "Not knowing, therefore, what he ought to believe about the Incarnation of the Divine Word, and not being willing to labor nor enlighten his mind from the breadth of the Holy Scripture, he might at least by paying careful attention have learned the common and uniform profession of faith which all the faithful make." He then went on to state some of the questioned elements of that faith: "They believe in one God, the Father Almighty, and in Jesus Christ, His only Son our Lord, who was born of the Holy Spirit and the Virgin Mary. It is by these three ideas that the machinations of almost all heretics are destroyed."

The rest of the "tome" is an authoritative, authentic description of Christian faith. Its merit is that it finally silenced the confusion that had so long agitated the Church.

Leo wrote a great deal. His letters flew in all directions. Fortunately for us, we have copies of many of them. Apparently he sent copies to the papal archives. We also have a collection of his letters from those cities which saved the originals sent to them. Leo's letters show another side to his work. Not all, not even the majority of his writings, were doctrinal correctives. A good deal of his time was spent in administration. For example, in his Letter No. 66 we see Leo writing to a group of bishops and priests. He is exercising his authority as head of the Church to remove some bishop and settle him in another see. The letter shows us Leo's discretion, prudence and concern. He knows that there has been an abuse of authority, and his reaction to it is swift but also kind and considerate. In removing the bishop, Leo writes, to save the honor of the people and their shepherd: "We do not permit the city of Vienne to go completely without honor as far as ecclesiastical jurisdiction is concerned, since in the acquiring of its privilege it is backed by the fact that it was we who previously made this arrangement. We do not want it to appear that the bishop has been suddenly demoted." Therefore, Leo finds a new place of dignity for the bishop and a new bishop for the disquieted see.

Letter No. 67 shows us another example of Leo's moderation and discretion. Not every instruction he gave was a written one. In writing to the bishop involved, he notes: "There are, however, many matters which are not to be put down in a letter. When you have learned of this from the report of our sons already named, you will carry them out efficiently and laudably, as we mentioned, with the Lord's assistance."

Even this brief sampling shows us that Leo was well aware of his authority and of how it had to be used. Aside from the kind words and considerate proposals, Leo speaks with direct authority, and his letters are filled with indisputable commands. He could not be unaware that he was building a new and universal administration that was offering the only alternative to a collapsing government.

In his role as the one who was trying to conserve some element of the fading Roman world, Leo is probably best remembered. Legend has clouded his encounter with Attila and the role he played as savior of the city. More likely than not, Leo and Attila met outside of Rome's walls to discuss how the sack of Rome could best be avoided. The military and civilian officials were useless. Attila had pillaged the north and central part of Italy. His Huns were now at Rome's door. Leo mounted a mule and made his way to the meeting with the Hun. We know not the content of that private conversation. But Attila was induced to leave. Some settlement had been worked out to spare Rome and its people. Fifteen hundred years later, Pius XII was to meet the Hun again to save Rome. The German forces were convinced as they withdrew to let Rome be declared an open city. This was the twilight of World War II, and the holocaust of a bombardment was spared the Eternal City. To this day both Popes are commemorated in Rome. In the nave of St. Peter's Basilica there is an altar above which stands a huge mosaic commemorating Leo and his meeting. In the square in front of St. Peter's Basilica stands a plaque put up by the City of Rome commemorating Pius XII's role as "savior of the city."

If Leo the Great was the man who saved some order from a crumbling world and gave some organization to a growing Church, Gregory the Great was the man who built on both and opened the way to a new world.

Gregory became Pope 150 years after Leo. There had been precious few "saviors of the city" in the intervening years. The city had been sacked four times and conquered with a regularity which denied any rebuilding. Damaged by fire, vandalism and earthquake, Rome was a dark and dreary city on the banks of the Tiber, shriveled from its once imperial size to less than 100,000 people.

This was the city into which was born Gregory. He was Roman. His father was Roman and some sort of a civil official. Gregory's genius can perhaps be seen in the varied career he enjoyed. At one point he is prefect of the city — the highest civil post in Rome. In this capacity he was mayor, sheriff and chief judge. We find he is also wealthy due to his training and commercial skills. Still later we find him named the ambassador to the Eastern Empire.

It seems that the stay in the East had a permanent effect on Gregory. On his return to Rome he entered a monastery. He lived a rigid monastic life for several years until he eventually became Pope.

The Tiber River overflowed its banks with a certain regularity. It carried with it debris, dirt and sickness. (This, in fact, continued up until the 1930s, when a retaining wall was built.) During one of these periodic floods, plague broke out in Rome. Among the victims carried off by the capricious Tiber was Pope Pelagius II.

Gregory found himself elected Pope. In this period of plague, as chief shepherd of the city Gregory organized a procession of prayers to plead for the health of the people. The legend surrounding the Castel Sant'Angelo tells us that at the height of the procession, an angel with a flaming sword appeared over the castle to drive out the plague. We do not know much about the legend or its foundation, but to this day, standing at the pinnacle of the old Mausoleum of Hadrian is still the great angel with his raised sword.

Another legend involves Gregory. Either before or after becoming Pope, he is said to have encountered a group of Angles from the islands that make up Great Britain. He is reported to have remarked, noting their flaxen hair and fine complexions, that they were angels, not Angles, and should belong to the Church of Christ. The legend at this point divides into two versions. According to one version, he himself set off to convert them. In this version he was not yet Pope. However, the people stopped him at the city gates because they could not bear to have him leave. The second version says that he was already

141

Pope and sent Augustine. Whatever truth there is to be found in the legends, the fact remains that Augustine was commissioned by Gregory to go to Britain and preach the faith. Augustine went, had great success, was eventually named the first Archbishop of Canterbury, and established a teaching tradition in that see city which endured for a thousand years.

As Augustine left Rome, he carried with him one of Gregory's great contributions: the *Regula Pastoralis,* a handbook for bishops. It explained the pastoral office of a bishop. In simple, clear, prudent terms, Gregory showed his brothers in the teaching office how to go about their work. This little volume, which was circulated throughout Italy, now found its way to Britain. Later, Alfred the Great was to translate this book. From England it made its way into the hands of Charlemagne. Charlemagne imposed it on all of the bishops of his realm and saw to it that it was the instructing manual for every bishop. In this strange sequence of events, Gregory's ideas became the foundation of learning and pastoral guidance for all of those bishops who held together civilization in Europe and built what came to be the nations of the modern world. There is no possible way of exaggerating the influence of this single work of Gregory.

But while his ecclesiastical affairs took up much time, other events were occupying Gregory. He had a huge relief program on his hands. Rome then, as now, is not capable of supplying the food it needs for the population it has. To Gregory fell the lot of keeping the supply lines, particularly from Sicily, open. He was now responsible for the entire civil government of Rome and its province. From police duties to street cleaning, all of these things became part of the work of the Bishop of Rome. He was also charged with the defense of the city. From Hadrian's wall in Britain to the banks of the Danube, civil administration faltered and order disappeared. Only the Church, in effect, remained. To her and her bishops (some of whom came to be called "prince-bishops"), fell the task of rebuilding society. No one else was there who could. With great gusto these men set to work. They became the protectors of the flock and civil administrators of their goods as well as guardians of their souls. Where food was needed, they supplied it. Where war was waged, many times they commanded. Minting money, levying taxes and reclaiming the land took their place as clerical duties alongside the administration of the sacraments and the Sunday sermon. This approach was climaxed in the reign of Innocent III (whose pontificate also gave Europe both St. Dominic and St. Francis of Assisi); Europe again found some semblance of political as well as spiritual unity.

Most historians agree that such a situation arose not because the priest went looking for public office and power. It became his lot, since he alone could read and write. Even those interpreters of history hostile to the Catholic tradition recognize that without the stopgap intervention of bishops and abbots, Western civilization as we know it could never have existed. Someone had to fill a vacuum created by total collapse.

The two "Greats," Leo and Gregory, worked to give the world a fresh start. Rome was gone. But the future still had to be lived. What Leo set out to do was to save what could be saved of the old and prepare a foundation for the new. Gregory took up his predecessor's work. He added the vision of a Church growing to encompass all men. He saw unity in faith replacing political agreement. On the foundations of Leo, Gregory by word, deed, teaching and example, opened the doors from Roman Europe on to a new Christian world — a world one in belief. He opened a door that led to Charlemagne, Christian Europe, the great universities, the monastic orders, the first hospitals, orphanages, schools, relief stations, libraries, musical revival — and a century of scholarship, theological, philosophical and legal, to which the world is still indebted to this day.

With Leo and Gregory, the age of the Fathers closed. But with them opened the great age of Doctors, saints, religious orders and a millennium of Christian unity.